breathe

breathe

Creating Space for God in a Hectic Life

Keri Wyatt Kent

Grand Rapids, Michigan

© 2005 by MOPS International

Published by Fleming H. Revell
a division of Baker Publishing Group
P.O. Box 6287, Grand Rapids, MI 49516-6287

Third printing, September 2005

Printed in the United States of America

Library of Congress Cataloging-in-Publication Data
Kent, Keri Wyatt, 1963–
    Breathe : creating space for God in a hectic life / Keri Wyatt Kent.
       p.   cm.
    Includes bibliographical references.
    ISBN 0-8007-3060-7 (pbk.)
    1. Christian women—Religious life. I. Title.
 BV4527.K455 2005
 248.8′43—dc22   2005001692

Unless otherwise indicated, Scripture is taken from the HOLY BIBLE, NEW INTERNATIONAL VERSION®. NIV®. Copyright © 1973, 1978, 1984 by International Bible Society. Used by permission of Zondervan. All rights reserved.

Scripture marked KJV is taken from the King James Version of the Bible.

Scripture marked Message is taken from *The Message* by Eugene H. Peterson, copyright © 1993, 1994, 1995, 2000, 2001, 2002. Used by permission of NavPress Publishing Group. All rights reserved.

Scripture marked NLT is taken from the *Holy Bible*, New Living Translation, copyright © 1996. Used by permission of Tyndale House Publishers, Inc., Wheaton, Illinois 60189. All rights reserved.

Published in association with the literary agency of Alive Communications, Inc., 7680 Goddard Street, Suite 200, Colorado Springs, CO 80920.

For Sibyl,

whose loving wisdom has influenced
so many of the life stories told in this book
(especially mine). With your words and with your life,
you are always reminding me that I have all the time
I need to do what God has called me to do.

contents

Part 5 The Reassurance

acknowledgments

This project would not have been possible without the support and encouragement of several key people:

First, my husband, Scot, and my children, Melanie and Aaron, who gave me time and space to write.

Bob Gordon, who edited the manuscript and somehow managed to be both brutally honest and incredibly encouraging.

My agent, Chip MacGregor, who patiently guided and encouraged me through the whole process.

Finally, all the women who bravely told me their stories, who shared the struggles and triumphs of their journey toward Sabbath Simplicity—thank you.

introduction

We have hints that there is a way of life vastly richer and deeper than all this hurried existence, a life of unhurried serenity and peace and power. If only we could slip over into that Center!

Thomas Kelly, *A Testament of Devotion*[1]

Thomas Kelly wrote those words about his own life in 1941, but he could have written them about my life this week. Hurry, I guess, is not new. Ours is not the first generation to feel that longing for a less frantic way of life. Like others before me, and maybe like you, I had a busy week:

Driving three hours each way for a one-hour speaking engagement. Helping my daughter study for a test. Taking the dog to the groomer. Cleaning, laundry, cleaning, laundry. Walking the dog. Trying to squeeze in a workout or two. Driving the soccer practice car pool. Listening to my kids as they sort out the challenges of an ordinary day. Working on this manuscript. Preparing for my next speaking gig, a retreat that starts the day after tomorrow. Answering emails, returning phone calls, planning and cooking meals. (I use that term broadly, hoping that frozen pizza does indeed count as a meal, especially if I put it in the oven for a while and serve it on plates rather than serving it straight out of the box.)

Center? Oh, sure, that would be nice, to live from the Center. But sometimes I feel so far on the edge that I have no idea where Center is, much less how to live there!

Kelly continued by writing, "We have seen and known some people who seem to have found this deep Center of living, where the fretful calls of life are integrated, where no as well as yes can be said with confidence."[2]

Fretful calls I am very familiar with. Seems like every time I turn around, I'm getting a fretful call, be it on the telephone or just one of my kids yelling "Mommmm!" My life is hectic because I have said yes to things that I should have said no to. That's fairly clear. But how do I say no? How do I get from where I am to the "Center"?

I have been trying for a decade to slow my life down. I have been writing about it, thinking about it, even speaking in public from a three-point outline telling other people how to do it. Still, I don't feel I've gotten very far on this journey toward simplicity and a slower pace of life. My effort to slow down and simplify is about the only thing in my life that is moving slowly!

Sometimes it seems to be working. Other times I feel like Wile E. Coyote after he goes over the cliff and paws frantically at the air, trying to slow himself while falling to the canyon floor. Slow down? I've got gravity to contend with here, and nothing I do is going to slow me down.

Despite my efforts to slow down, my life—crowded with work, kids, activities, and obligations—is sometimes hurried. I don't like this. I really do want to slow down; I want to catch my breath. I feel sucked into a vortex of busyness, and frankly, I don't like it one bit. I want to have enough space in my schedule to do something spontaneous without having to schedule it two weeks in advance. That's as close as I come to spontaneous these days.

I am writing this book, in part, because I want to learn more about how to live at a saner pace. Why? Because the pace of our lives has profound implications upon the depth of our lives. I don't want to just skim the surface of life; I want to have deep and meaningful relationships with my family, my friends, God. And this I do know: you can't love in a hurry.

When my life gets too crowded, what gets crowded out? Usually, it's spiritual pursuits—my relationship with God and my ability to stay "centered" on him. It's not just that hurry makes us stressful. It's that when we hurry, we lose touch with God and all he wants to give us.

In writing this book, I talked with a number of women who were hurried. I wondered what motivated them to be so busy and found that they were motivated by many of the same things I was. I also talked with some women who appear to have found "a way of life vastly richer and deeper," and I want to know how in *this* world they did that!

That's what this book is about: how to stop being so hurried . . . to live in the moment . . . to connect with God . . . to simply be. It's about how to practice simplicity, how to slow down, and more importantly, why we would want to practice those things.

Sounds nice. But it's not easy. We've got busy schedules and hectic hearts. How did we ever get so hurried?

The journey has been different for each of us, but many of the pressures we've faced are the same. The pressure to keep up, to succeed, whether it's in our career or in the way we parent, or both. We want to have our children succeed and do well. We feel some pressure to be what feels like Superwoman or maybe Super Mom. We know we can't, and we usually even say we can't. Yet our actions say something else. How did that happen?

I'm guessing it's because hurry is normal.

Multitasking, a word we didn't even know a decade ago, is normal. I'm not Superwoman, you insist, I'm every woman. Everyone lives like this, unless they are members of some religious order tucked away in a monastery or are living off the land in Idaho. Or are, perhaps, Amish.

Yet maybe not. Maybe there is a way to live that is not so frantic. Maybe it's possible to find this "deep Center" and live from it. But how do you construct such a life?

Do you ever feel that simplifying and centering your life sounds like more work, and as tired and busy as you are, you can't possibly squeeze in one more thing, even something that might bring peace?

Wouldn't it be amazing if you could live your life in such a way that you had room for the things that mattered: deep relationships with people, a strong and vital connection with God, rejuvenating rest and recreation? Wouldn't it be great if you could just have some room to breathe?

The fact is, such a life is available. You truly can slow down and have that kind of life. I've talked at length with women who—despite kids, jobs, and incredible peer pressure to keep busy all the time—have found a simpler way of life. There *is* an alternative to being hurried. It *is* possible to simplify your life, to connect with God deeply. As I said before, I've been working on it for ten years, and though it's hard to see progress at times, I do think I've made some. The moms whose stories I've included have also made quite a bit of progress.

I've met a lot of women who need to slow down more than I do, which makes me feel better in a demented sort of way. Some of them were even willing to share their stories with me for this book, and to admit that they suffer from a hurry addiction, or at least that they have a lot of trouble saying no.

I've also found some women who have really simplified, and in so doing have discovered that "deep Center of living" that Thomas Kelly writes of so eloquently. I've included their stories too, to show that this whole learning how to breathe and slow down is a process, not a one-day project. My conversations with them also helped me to learn what my next step is in this journey toward a simpler life.

Unfortunately, each person I've met who lives simply, who practices simplicity, does it differently. That figures, doesn't it? I guess simplicity isn't that simple.

I did notice some trends, some common themes, though, in the stories of women who had slowed down. They've addressed, each in their own unique way, three practices: slowing, simplicity, and Sabbath-keeping. In other words, their pace, their focus, and their rhythm of life were all congruent. They live a life of what I call Sabbath Simplicity: a God-focused life rhythm of work and rest.

Sabbath Simplicity is not something you add to a crowded life; it's a way of life that you build by listening to God's direction. It's living from that Center in a deliberate but almost effortless way. It's choosing what to say yes to and what to say no to based not on the demands or example of others but on what God is calling you to.

In his teachings on how to live, Jesus often issued an invitation to simply do life with him. One such invitation, found in Matthew 11:28–30, is woven through the chapters of this book: "Come to me, all you who are weary and burdened, and I will give you rest. Take my yoke upon you and learn from me, for I am gentle and humble in heart, and you will find rest for your souls. For my yoke is easy and my burden is light."

Could it be possible to find real rest? Could the life he invites us into actually be light and easy? Could we actually take Jesus up on his invitation?

I believe it is possible . . . and here is why. When Jesus spoke of his "yoke," his listeners in that day and culture would understand it a bit differently than we might. A rabbi like Jesus would tell his followers how he interpreted the Torah (the first five books of our Bible) and the Prophets. His interpretation of how to apply God's law, how to live it out, was called his yoke.

For example, a rabbi's yoke was simply his teaching on what it means, practically speaking, to "love your neighbor" or "honor your parents." What specific things did you need to do to comply with those rules? And which rules were the most important? That's what a rabbi's yoke addressed. A rabbi's disciples would take on his yoke, that is, try to emulate their master, try to live out God's law by using the rabbi as a role model. That's why, in the gospel stories, you often find people asking Jesus questions such as "Which is the most important commandment?" or "Who is my neighbor?" They are asking, okay, Jesus, what's your yoke?

Learning this (thanks to Pastor Rob Bell) was revolutionary for me. I had always thought of a yoke as a heavy burden, and I was confused about how a yoke could be easy or light. If a yoke is simply a way of life, a lifestyle that Jesus modeled, a way of life that says simply love God and love each other, then it is entirely possible it could be something light. This way of life is what I mean by Sabbath Simplicity.

The metaphor also reminds us that we are not working by ourselves. Instead, we are yoked to Jesus, and he shares equally in the burden of our transformation. He is at our side and is for us. We're not carrying the burden of living the Christian life alone. Jesus is not the farmer driving the ox; he's the other ox pulling with us. We need to slow down enough to notice that he's there and work with him, not against him.

Jesus's words in Matthew 11:28–30 provide the framework for this book. I've broken his invitation into phrases. Each phrase heads up two chapters, focused on the idea or invitation in that phrase. Each chapter begins with the story of a real-life mom (whose name has been changed). These stories will provide a picture of real people on the real journey toward Sabbath Simplicity. As you will see, some are just beginning that journey, and others have traveled a long way and have much to teach all of us.

Dallas Willard once wrote that the secret of the easy yoke is to live your life as Jesus would if he were in your place. How do you do that? I believe the first step is to slow down the pace. That allows you to be fully present, to be mindful, to be intentional, to create space, and to notice where God is working and join him in that work.

This book will focus on three Christian practices that help us live as Jesus would if he were in our place: simplicity, slowing, and Sabbath-keeping. Pay attention as you read, though. Notice that these three create space for practices such as solitude, service, prayer, meditation on Scripture, and others. I have focused on these three because if we simply pray more or read the Bible faster, we will never find the secret of the easy yoke. Any spiritual practice, from solitude to service, must be approached in an unhurried fashion, or the benefits of the practice itself will be lost. Connection with God, which is the reason for any spiritual practice, begins with changing our focus (from ourselves and our problems to God and his sufficiency) and changing our pace (from hurried and distracted to deliberate and focused). That is what simplicity, slowing, and Sabbath-keeping force us to do. They move us toward a life, an easy yoke, which if you let it, will open up space for God. That is the reason for this book: to direct you toward a simpler lifestyle with more of God in it and to help you find rest for your soul and lighten your burden.

I know you are busy. But please don't skim this book. Read it slowly. If you find yourself speed-reading a book on slowing down, ponder the irony of that. If you can't see the irony, you need more than this book. You need therapy.

Even the chapters are designed to make you pause, to create space. As you read, you will encounter interruptions in the form of boxes labeled "Breathing Exercise." When you get to one of these, stop and think! Don't skip it! Stop, take a deep breath. Even if you are reading the book while waiting at the pediatrician's office or on the soccer field sidelines or in the bathtub after the kids are in bed, take just a few moments and try the exercise. Then when you finish the chapter, set aside some time to go back and try the Breathing Exercises again before moving on to the next chapter. You may want to record some of your observations in a journal as you read and explore the exercises.

I write not as an expert but as a fellow traveler. Before having children, I was a reporter for a large daily newspaper. I learned to observe, to ask questions, to write about the things I learned. This book will offer insights based on conversations with real women living real lives, and taking steps toward a simpler, less hurried life.

Take a deep breath and come along with us on the journey.

part one

the invitation

Come to me, all you who are
weary and burdened,
and I will give you rest

1

hurried and worried

How did I get here?

Jane is the mother of five children. (Yes, five!) The oldest is eight, the youngest, two. (Do the math: five kids in six years!) Jane works outside the home twenty-five to thirty hours a week and is a member of the PTA at her children's school, where she also spends several hours a week volunteering. She helps organize lots of neighborhood activities, from the bowling league to Bunco nights. But the thing that really keeps her busy is her children's schedule.

Her three oldest children are each involved in two or three sports, which often means up to a dozen games or practices each week. This makes her carpooling schedule, well, challenging. She's very good at juggling and sharing rides with other moms, but she does her share of driving for not only her kids but other people's as well.

The two oldest children also take piano lessons. She wants them to do well, so each night after dinner she sits down and oversees their practicing and also makes sure they have done their homework. They have faith class every week at church too.

Jane has started trying to learn more about the Bible by attending a neighborhood study group. She often fits in an early morning jog before her husband leaves for work, which she says not only helps her stay in shape but relieves stress.

Jane is either crazy or Wonder Woman; I'm not sure which. Right now some of you are saying, "Don't tell me any more about this woman. She makes the rest of us look bad." Which is true, if the goal of life is to do as much as you can as fast as you can. But is that the goal?

Because she has a flexible job, an excellent and dependable babysitter (who drives and can handle five kids), and her mother living nearby, Jane is often able to keep all the plates spinning. However, she's found that things like one of the children getting sick or the holiday season arriving puts her into survival mode. "I'm just trying to get through December," she told me two weeks before Christmas.

Adding an event to the already crammed schedule makes things extremely hectic as well. A recent wedding (three of the children were participating in it!) during baseball season meant two baseball games and a rehearsal dinner Friday night and nine different obligations on Saturday.

Despite her busy schedule, Jane is really good at just stopping to enjoy a moment. She's the first one to play kickball or tag with the kids at the park. She recently had a summer Saturday without any activities in it. Rather than plan an excursion or schedule something, she let her kids play in the backyard and enjoy the day. Just letting the day unfold was a step toward simplicity.

What do you think about Jane and her life? Do you think, "I don't know how she does that, or for that matter, why she does it. It sounds exhausting." Or, do you say, "That's nothing. You should see *my* family's schedule."

Most likely, you fall somewhere in the middle. You can identify, but maybe your calendar's not quite as packed as Jane's. Maybe it's just as packed, but *your* mom lives out of state. Most of us—if we're not like Jane—probably know someone like her.

The Hurried Woman

Jesus was talking to me, and Jane, and a lot of other women, when he called to those who are "weary." In our culture, weary is a way of life.

Dr. Brent W. Bost, an obstetrician-gynecologist in Beaumont, Texas, says there are sixty million women in America who are so overscheduled and overstressed that it affects their physical health. Dr. Bost has written a book (*The Hurried Woman Syndrome*), has a website (www.hurried woman.com), and has been on countless TV shows talking about this problem.

These women, he says, experience chronic fatigue or even mild depression, weight gain (whether we eat to comfort ourselves or to raise our energy level), and not surprisingly, a lack of interest in sex. His diagnosis: Hurried Woman Syndrome. A Q&A on his website quotes the doctor as saying:

> Stress is probably the single most important factor that causes women to complain about the Hurried Woman Syndrome. There are many types of stress and they vary from patient to patient. Sometimes the stress can't be avoided, such as a sick child or a high-powered career. However, for

the majority of women, much of the stress is avoidable or at least could be managed better. These avoidable stresses are those that often come from a busy, hectic schedule and lifestyle choices that many of us have embraced as completely "normal." Yet, the effects of this kind of stress—what I call "hurry"—can have very significant long-term and wide-reaching consequences for the woman who labors under it and those around her who suffer along with her.[1]

Despite the fact that a doctor is telling us that hurry will cause us to feel fatigued or depressed, gain weight, and lose interest in sex, we still find it hard to slow down. Why? I think it is in part because we believe the lie that "if I am busy, I must be important."

Also, as Dr. Bost has observed (along with the rest of us), hurry has become normal. Feeling overwhelmed has become normal. Many of us respond to that overwhelmed feeling by eating more. Or we eat fast food too often and say we are too busy to exercise. No matter what our excuse, Americans are heavier than they've ever been. Gaining weight is normal.

Judging by the number of Americans taking antidepressants, it seems that depression is almost normal, or at least more common.

And loss of interest in sex (perhaps due to exhaustion) is almost par for the course, especially for parents of young children. Or at least, such a trend that it makes the cover of *Newsweek*. The June 30, 2003, cover showed a couple in their jammies sitting in bed, looking anything but romantic, under the headline "No Sex, Please, We're Married: Are Stress, Kids and Work Killing Romance?" Most working moms would respond, "Well, duh! Of course." The article says basically that the answer to that question for couples with young children, especially if both are working, is yes.

Breathing Exercise

Do you exhibit any of the symptoms of Hurried Woman Syndrome (fatigue or depression, weight gain, or decreased libido)? Are these symptoms related to the pace of your life? Take a few moments to look through your day timer or palm pilot. Are your days hurried?

This evening, before you go to sleep, try a classic spiritual practice called a review of the day. Simply go back over your day as if you were watching yourself on video. Where did you go? Did you feel hurried as you went? Whom did you see and talk to? Did you interact with others in a loving way, whether family, friends, or strangers? Were you patient or did you feel stressed? Did you notice God anywhere in your day?

If you try this simple practice for a few days, patterns may reveal themselves. Has hurry become normal for you? How is this affecting you emotionally, relationally, physically, spiritually?

Urgency and Productivity

Let's face it: multitasking has become normal. We squeeze in as much as we can—and much of it at the same time! We think doing several things at once will help us finish our to-do list. Unfortunately, it doesn't. If we try to do two things at once, we have trouble giving full concentration to either task. For example, many car accidents are caused by people trying to drive and talk on the phone simultaneously. Because drivers are distracted by conversations, they can't give their full concentration to driving.

Also, productivity and efficiency tests have shown that workers who work for fifty minutes an hour and then take a ten-minute break are more productive than those who work sixty minutes without a break. And the difference in their productivity goes up the more hours they work. Those who take regular breaks actually get more done than those who work unceasingly. So taking breaks will help us get more done.

But certainly, life is about more than productivity, more than quantifiable results. We desire a better quality of life as well.

We want it, but we don't make the connection between speed and stress. Or we kind of see it, in the peripheral vision of our lives, but we don't see it clearly enough to change things. We think we don't have time to even stop and wonder why we're so rushed. At times, hurry feels so normal we're not even aware we have a problem or how we might possibly begin to address the problem if we were to notice or admit to it.

I am aware of the impact of hurry on my life. I know how I want to live, but I can't do it. I'm too busy. I try not to be hurried, but I'm too hurried to even realize how hurried I am!

If you are feeling stressed and think it may have something to do with the speed of your life, you need to know how to change it. This matters. We fool ourselves when we think it doesn't. Yes, we admit, we may feel some stress, but we figure if we are not experiencing the symptoms that Dr. Bost describes—if we're managing and hanging in there—we must be okay, right?

Probably not. A hurried life may contribute to other health problems as well. A 2003 Northwestern University study of more than three thousand men and women suggests that people who spend their twenties racing to find time or who are impatient to "get moving" are twice as likely to have high blood pressure down the line than people who move at a slower pace (from www.savon .com).

The study linked the so-called type A personality— the hard-driving, take-charge, win-at-all-costs personality—with hypertension. As a person's "time urgency" increased, so did his or her blood pressure. To determine people's time urgency, they were asked questions such as:

Do you often get very upset if you are forced to wait for something?

Do you usually feel pressured about time?

Do you feel you don't have enough time at the end of a workday?

Do you feel you don't have enough time during the day?

Based on the answers to those questions, people were ranked according to five categories ranging from those who had absolutely no sense of time urgency (the folks we might label as sluggish or lazy) to those with high time urgency, who, like the White Rabbit in *Alice in Wonderland* are always racing about checking their watches. The latter had more health problems than those who moved at a slower pace.

Breathing Exercise

Look at the time urgency questions above. Spend some time journaling as you answer each one. Add the question "Why?" to the end of each, as in, "Do you usually feel pressured about time? Why?" On a scale of one to ten, what would you say your time urgency is? What factors contribute to that? How does your time urgency level affect your health? Your relationships? Your spiritual life?

Do you ever find yourself hurrying even when you are doing things that don't need to be done fast, like praying or spending time with your spouse or children?

A Healthy Soul

So, maybe now you're thinking you ought to put the book down and go get your blood pressure checked? It gets worse. Physical health concerns are just part of the picture of the damage hurry can do to our lives.

Hurry will damage not only your mind and your body, but it will wreak havoc on your soul as well. How is the health of your soul? Do you feed your spirit good things? Do you exercise the part of you that is most truly and deeply *you*? Answer this: Are you deeply satisfied with your spiritual life? Do you feel a sense of peace and God's presence most of the time? Once in a while? Ever?

I am not trying to make you feel guilty about missing your "quiet time" or taking a week off from church. God's not interested in your religious activities as much as he is interested in an intimate soul connection with you. I often say I want that intimacy with God, but then several days will slip by and I won't have spent any time being still; I won't have connected with God.

Most of us would probably not consciously say, "I could spend deeply meaningful time with God or I could run around like a maniac. Hmm. I think I'll be a maniac." But by not slowing down, by saying yes to overscheduling or the demands of others, that is what we're saying in effect. The trouble is, we don't even think about the choices we make. That's why we end up doing things we really don't want to do.

As much as you may think you want that intimacy with your heavenly Father, if you keep yourself too busy, you will squeeze that relationship to the edges of your life. It can happen whether you are too busy with your kids and home, your career, or even doing "religious" things like teaching Sunday school or doing your homework for Bible study.

When we live life in a hurry, we end up weary . . . in a hurry. For me, the weariness means that I might let things slide a little. I will show up for the third volunteer opportunity I've said yes to this week, but I may not have a good attitude or even do a good job.

But you need to know this: it is possible to slow down. You can do it. And you don't have to wait until you burn out. You just have to recognize the problem and notice what it's doing to your soul.

Slowing for many of us begins when we hear Jesus say, "Come to me, all you who are weary and burdened, and I will give you rest" (Matt. 11:28). He does not say, "Come to me, all you who are perfect and have no problems." He offers rest for the weary, true spiritual rest that refreshes us and connects us with him. We don't have to pull ourselves together. He meets us in the midst of our weariness, in our place of weakness.

How do we "come to Jesus"? It's not just about having faith or praying a prayer. Those are key steps, but if we don't slow down, we won't stick with our relationship with him.

Pastor and author John Ortberg writes that his mentor, Dallas Willard, advised him that if he wanted to grow spiritually, he needed to "ruthlessly eliminate hurry" from his life. Not just slow down a little bit, but ruthlessly eliminate hurry. Not just occasionally, but from our lives. Our whole lives. Ortberg notes: "Hurry is the great enemy of the spiritual life in our day. Hurry can destroy our souls. Hurry can keep us from living well."[2] In other words, hurry becomes a barrier to deeper connection with God.

Knowing this, you'd think we would just slow down. We'd do anything we could to live a life of Sabbath Simplicity. But we don't. Why?

What Drives You?

The reasons for keeping ourselves busy are many. Jane chooses to offer her five children the chance to try all sorts of sports and activities because she never had that opportunity. Her childhood looked a little different. She went to work in the family business while still in grade school. Her weekends, evenings, and summers were consumed with working. She longs to give her children a different sort of childhood.

Some of us have other reasons for keeping ourselves, and our children, busy. We might hope to see our unrealized ambitions achieved through our children. Or we might simply be responding to subtle peer pressure: this is what all the other people we know are doing, so it's what we must do. We've never stopped to consider that there might be an alternative to the hectic schedules we keep.

We are running—and running hard. The logical question becomes, What are we running from? Or what are we running to? Sometimes we are running from the past. We feel guilt over past mistakes, be they youthful indiscretions of a decade or more ago or the way we carelessly hurt a friend's feelings last week. So rather than face these things, we just get busy. But if our past is motivating us, we are not living in the present. We are not in the moment, and we are missing the gifts of this day.

Sometimes we are running forward, hoping to achieve something. If we can only earn so much money, we'll have arrived. If our kids make this team or win that championship, they will be popular, and we will bask in the glow of their accomplishments.

If you are an at-home parent, you likely have had people ask, "What do you do all day?" Keeping overly busy allows us to fight off the demons of inadequacy that attack when people ask us that question. Perhaps you give more detail than people really want:

"Well, I had to drop off the dry cleaning and walk the dog (while pushing the stroller, of course). Then I took the baby to a friend's and went to the older children's school for two hours, volunteering in the computer lab. I picked up the baby (he napped in the car), and then I ran through the grocery store and then home, let the dog out, packed snacks for the kids, picked them up at school, took Stephanie to her piano lesson and Joey to his soccer practice, went back and got Stephanie from piano and took her to gymnastics (with a brief detour through the drive-through window at McDonald's so she could eat on the way), and then went back and got Joey, took him home to start his homework and have something to eat. Thank God Susan's mother could drive Stephanie home from gymnastics, or I would have been really busy!"

It's as if we believe that our value comes from what we do. And why shouldn't we think that? It's the message of our culture. The only problem is, it's a lie! Our value comes not from what we do but from who we are. And we are beloved children of God. The Bible reminds us, "How great is the love the Father has lavished on us, that we should be called children of God! And that is what we are!" (1 John 3:1). God loves me, and his love is not stingy or limited. He gives it lavishly, generously, enough that it makes me who I am.

Breathing Exercise

As a parent, how do you feel about your children? What, specifically, do you love about each of them? Do you love them for their accomplishments or just because of who they are—your kids? Put aside any frustrations you may have experienced with your children today. Sit with that feeling of love for a minute or two. Then read 1 John 3:1 again. As much as you love your children, God loves you even more. He lavishes love upon you, not because of your good behavior but because of his grace toward you, his child. Take a moment to enjoy God's love for you.

A Complicated World

Another reason it is hard to slow down is that technological change continues to occur at an ever-increasing pace. Dealing with such rapid change is stressful. Even in the last ten to twenty years, things have changed dramatically. When we were children, our parents didn't have cell phones, email, or voice mail. An answering machine was cutting edge.

We live in a hectic world, where everyone around us seems to keep moving faster. I'm often amazed at the time just being the administrator of my own life requires.

Life in the last one hundred years has become infinitely more complicated. My grandmother was born in 1901. She never drove a car; when cars became commonplace, she relied on her husband or one of her sisters if she needed a ride. She lived in a small town in New Jersey where she could walk or take the bus to the market or her sisters' houses (they all lived nearby). She did a lot of walking, which may be part of the reason she lived to be ninety-eight.

She saw vast changes in her lifetime. For example, look at one small thing: keeping the house warm in winter. My grandmother, as a child, lived in a house without central heat. Winters were survived by keeping fires burning in a fireplace and a large Franklin stove in the kitchen. To warm the sheets at night, they used hot water bottles, or metal bins filled with hot coals from the fire, then smoothed over the sheets. She and one or more of her sisters often shared a bed for the sake of warmth.

The home she raised her children in had a coal furnace. My grandparents bought the coal from a coal man who came to their house. The coal man did not telemarket or send junk mail. He knocked on their door. There were not five different coal men offering various prices or package deals.

Back then, if you had enough money to buy coal, you had heat. If not, you burned what you could and warmed yourself at the cookstove, using the fuel for both heating and cooking.

This week, by comparison, I have received three telemarketing calls offering me a way to change the billing on my natural gas supply so I can take advantage of prices as low as sixty-eight cents per therm. I'm assuming a therm is a unit of measurement, but how big? I have absolutely no clue. And I also am in the dark as to whether sixty-eight cents is a bargain or highway robbery. The rate could go up if I don't lock in at this rate. But what if it goes down? I have central heat, for which I'm grateful, but the paperwork and decisions required to keep the heat on (and avoid feeling like I'm being ripped off) are not exactly simple.

I'm told the best way to keep costs low is to keep changing suppliers, be it for natural gas, insurance, telephone service, or whatever. All of this involves more paper than my grandmother's family burned heating their house on a cold day back in 1915. It also involves my time and interruptions like telemarketing calls. Just handling the details of life takes an inordinate amount of time and adds to my sense of hurry and distraction. I feel burdened by the paper that piles up, and I'm stressed because I don't know which long-distance plan really is the best deal or what a therm is.

We are bombarded with information and choices, and on top of that, we do indeed choose to be too busy; you can begin to see that we have put ourselves in a difficult situation.

God in the Margins

A hurried life not only affects our physical well-being but our spiritual health as well. If we move too fast, God gets put in the margins of our lives, squeezed to the sidelines.

I remember writing papers in high school. I love to write, but if I wasn't very enthused about an assigned topic, I would try to fill the requisite number of pages by double-spacing and leaving very generous margins. Wider margins meant fewer words per page, thus filling the required number of pages with fewer words. Of course, this allowed my teachers plenty of white space along the edges to write "you didn't fully develop this point" in red ink!

Remember airmail letters? (If you don't, ask your grandma.) In the days before email, you would send a letter overseas via airmail. You could buy special stationery for it at the post office. It was a one-page, tissue-thin blue paper that folded into an envelope. In order to get as much information as possible onto one page (and avoid extra postage charges), you would write small and fill every available space on the stationery.

My life feels a lot more like an airmail letter than a high school term paper. Sometimes it feels like there's information, thoughts, tasks, and obligations crammed into every available space. Just looking at it sort of stresses me. Yet at other times, I am able to keep the margins generous. I purposely don't allow my life to be cluttered; I ruthlessly prune my schedule and commitments. But unless I keep after it, I tend to forget, and I begin to think that the empty space is there to be filled with hectic activity. So I fill it again, sometimes consciously, often unconsciously.

What would happen to my life if I put God in the center of the page? If his influence and presence were seen in every sentence, in every note that I jot to myself? Sometimes my life gets so full—even with good things like family, work, and church activities—that the margins become exceedingly narrow. God gets the tiny leftover spaces, or he gets gently shoved off the page entirely. A hurried life is not just stressful; it pushes God out from the center of my life and puts him in the margins, which are airmail thin.

Richard Swenson is a physician who saw stress and burnout causing health problems with many of his patients. He wrote a book about how so-called "progress" has made the margins of modern life way too thin.

"Do you know families who feel drawn and quartered by overload? Do you know wage earners who are overworked, teachers who are overstressed, farmers who are overextended, pastors who are overburdened, or mothers of young children who are overwhelmed? Chances are the pathogen of marginless living is largely responsible."[3]

Spiritual growth comes from listening to God and responding to him in ways we might not have planned ahead of time. When there is no extra space in our lives, when we are living a "marginless life," we have no reserves. Marginless is quite similar to sleeplessness. As a mom, you may be quite familiar with that condition! You think to yourself, "I would be a much more patient and loving mother if only my kids would sleep through the night."

Getting enough sleep is one way of keeping enough margin in our lives. Of course, sometimes circumstances can't be helped. If you are up all night with a crying baby, you are not going to have the reserves to be Super Mom all day. Give yourself some grace. Be realistic about what you can accomplish. Sometimes restoring margin to your life means taking a much-needed nap.

Swenson also writes, "Margin is the amount allowed beyond that which is needed. It is something held in reserve for contingencies or unanticipated situations. Margin is the gap between rest and exhaustion, the space between breathing freely and suffocating. It is the leeway we once had between ourselves and our limits. Margin is the opposite of overload. If we are overloaded we have no margin, or we have negative margin. If however, we are careful to avoid overloading, margin reappears. Most people are not quite sure when they pass from margin to overload."[4]

How do you increase the margin in your everyday life? You have to first decide not to hurry. The younger your children are, the harder this is sometimes. The things that make you feel rushed and hurried change as your children develop. If your children are very small, you may not be rushing around in the car. You're rushing around the living room after a toddler who seems to have tornado genes in his DNA. Everything he tries to touch gets destroyed or at least moved out of place. Just keeping him from pulling the floor lamp down on his head takes a lot of your time. So you feel hurried but also as if you've done very little except prevent disasters.

If you have very small children, you will often find yourself feeling hurried because everything takes longer than you thought it would. You can begin to slow down when you expect the unexpected; leave earlier than you think you ought to when you try to go anywhere. Expect your infant to spit up in the car seat right after you buckle her in. Expect your son to take off the shoes you just put on his feet when you turn your back to grab his coat, even if he's excited that you are taking him to the park.

I am always amazed at how long it takes just to get out the door, even when the kids want to go wherever it is we're going. I need to stop being surprised . . . and so do you.

You have a couple of kids; you're going to have to allow twenty minutes from the time you start getting ready to leave until you actually leave. Plan more time than that if you have more children.

There are times we need to prod children to get going, but often we push them even if there is nowhere we have to be and absolutely no reason to hurry.

Practice building margin into your days. Try leaving five minutes earlier than you think you should when you go somewhere. Don't wait until you know that the only way you'll be on time is if every stoplight on the way there is green.

If we have margin in our lives, we can handle a few red lights. We might even have time to take a divine detour. We can look into the eyes of our co-worker and really listen, perhaps even offer a word of encouragement. We can actually enjoy a cuddle on the couch with our children. Sometimes divine detours happen when we extend ourselves and receive an unexpected blessing, as a friend of mine did recently.

Her father had just passed away, right before Christmas. She had been very close to him, and she missed him so much. She was trying to keep her chin up. After all, her father had always told her, "Keep smiling." Those days, though, it was hard to smile. On her way somewhere in the car, she saw a scruffy man, obviously homeless, walking down the road. She could have driven past, hurried on. Instead, she stopped. She pulled a $20 bill from her wallet and handed it out the car window to the man, wishing him a Merry Christmas.

"Thank you," he said. He looked right at her and smiled. "Keep smiling!" he said.

My friend could not believe what she'd heard. Why did a homeless man choose those words to thank her for her kindness? She asked me later what I thought.

"That's how God works," I told her. How many divine detours have you driven past today?

Sorting out and becoming aware of your motives, of what drives you, is a necessary step to slowing down your life. Identifying whatever barrier stands between you and a simpler, slower life is the first step to getting it out of your path. You *can* change. It is possible to "ruthlessly eliminate hurry." The result will be not just a slower life but also a more deeply satisfying one.

It is possible to simplify your life, to connect deeply with God. You can embrace Sabbath Simplicity not just as a good idea but as the lifestyle you live. But first you have to learn to breathe.

Breathing Exercise

Think of your life as a page. Is every inch covered? Does it have any empty space? How much margin is there in your life? Do you feel overloaded? How do you feel about this? What would you have to do to increase the margin in your life?

2

out of breath

How can I slow down?

Christine has four children: thirteen-year-old twins, an eleven-year-old, and a six-year-old. When the twins were born, she cut her hours at work from full- to part-time. Still, getting the kids to child care and herself to work was no easy task, as any working mother knows.

She'd drop them off at day care early in the morning on her way to work. "I would dress them in their clothes for the next day the night before, so they slept in their clothes. When they were babies it wasn't that big of a deal. I'd pull them out of their cribs in the morning and take them to day care," she recalls. "When I had the third one, I was trying to potty train twin two-year-olds and handle a newborn. Going to work was my sanity, actually. I'd have to pack the trunk of the car with bikes and toys to take to my mom's one day, my mother-in-law's the other, and day care a third day."

When her fourth child was born five years later, the older children were in a private school, which meant Christine had to drive them to school, get her youngest to day care, then go to work. She'd leave the house at 7:30 a.m. and not return until late in the day, because in addition to her job and the kids' school, they began to get involved in extracurricular activities like gymnastics and soccer.

"We would be driving all the time. The kids would do their homework in the car, and I'd think to myself, 'I can't believe I'm doing this.' One time, one of the kids got the other kid's head stuck in the sunroof. Other times, we'd be stuck in a snowstorm, and it would take hours to get them to school. By the time I got to work, I was worn out, and I found I was totally resenting my co-workers. They'd be complaining about something going on at the office and I'd think, 'You have no idea what I did just to get here.'"

Eventually Christine felt that the pressure of her job was too much. She decided to quit. This relieved a lot of pressure and enabled her to slow down. While it reduced the family income, she didn't have the expenses of child care and other work-related things (lunches out, dry cleaning, and so forth). She was able to simplify her life, cut expenses, and certainly slow down the pace. For a while.

But as the kids grew, they became more interested in sports. Christine felt like she had all the time in the world since she wasn't working outside of the house. And she had time to herself while the kids were in school. She enjoyed going to Bible study at church, volunteering at her children's school, and being able to run errands without four kids in tow.

Since she had "so much time" because she wasn't working, she quite willingly (if perhaps unwittingly) took on another job: that of chauffeur and manager for her children. A high-energy, driven person, Christine is aware that it's hard for her to stay slowed down.

These days, each of her four children is in at least two sports. One of the twins is becoming an accomplished gymnast, which means almost daily workouts, each several hours long. The other takes horseback riding lessons, which is also a more than once-a-week commitment; she also takes piano, but has to have her lesson at 8:30 p.m. because that's the only time she has available.

"I feel pressure from other parents," Christine says. "And, once you let one of your kids do travel soccer, you have to let the others do it. Now we've got our fourth child coming up; he's in first grade and on two soccer teams."

Opportunity for What?

If your children have athletic abilities and friends and coaches urge you to put them on the right team to "develop their potential," it's often hard to resist. Rather than just putting the children in a less competitive "recreational" league, parents will push kids (often as young as eight years old, or even younger) to try out for more competitive "travel" leagues, which means competitive try-outs just to make the team, more frequent and intense practices, and away games in other towns. All this creates more pressure on children and parents and takes up more of their time. It also means more car pools and sometimes driving an hour to get to a game.

In addition, a child who is naturally athletic often excels not just at one sport but at just about everything she tries. As a result, parents feel pressure to sign up for far too many sports. If a child is on a travel team for more than one sport, the miles on the minivan start to really add up, and the practice schedule can keep them busy every day of the week. That pressure is a burden, but Christine's not sure what to do with it.

"I've never told my kids they can't sign up for something when they asked to," Christine told me.

"Why not?" I asked.

"I don't know. Maybe I don't want to be at this pace, but I see it as an opportunity for them to build friendships with other kids, and if they want to play high school sports, they have to play on a travel team now."

I hear this from many parents. They have believed dire warnings from other parents that their child has to be at the top, they have to be on the right team in grade school or they won't make the cut in high school. Well, so what? What if they don't? Then they won't get a scholarship. Okay. That might be true. But what really drives us is that we think the opposite is true: if they are on the right team, they will make the high school team and then go on to get a college scholarship. I am here to tell you, odds are it's not going to happen like that.

Your child who has been playing competitive soccer (and three others sports besides!) since age four might make the high school team and she might not. If she does make the high school team, in our minds, she will automatically get a scholarship to play soccer for a good college. It's entirely possible that your child may enjoy high school sports, even do well, but not have colleges knocking on the door offering scholarships. Throw into the mix that children who have been pushed into competitive sports from age four will have been working their tails off for fourteen years by the time they graduate from high school. They may very well be so burned out by then that they won't even accept a scholarship, should one be offered.

Many coaches have told Christine that her children are excellent athletes. This type of comment messes with you as a parent. When your kids are small and just playing in a recreational or instructional league and a coach or other parents say, "Wow, they are really good. You ought to think about getting them on a travel team or club team," it's hard to say no. It sounds terrific. You wouldn't want to squelch that potential, right?

That's the kind of thinking that has resulted in Christine's four kids each having a practice or game (on top of homework) every night of the week. The kids enjoy athletics, but Christine's noticed that her thirteen-year-old's enthusiasm occasionally wanes. "Sometimes at games it seems like she's not even trying," Christine said.

I asked Christine, "What if you told her she didn't have to do this sport?"

"What would she do on Fridays then?" Christine asked me. She was serious.

I don't want to have my kids lie around every night in front of the television, but I do want them to have days where they can just hang out and play, or read, or daydream. Having to figure out on their own what to do with occasional unstructured afternoons provides kids a great developmental opportunity: learning how to manage their own time.

Christine says she wishes she and her husband had decided when their kids were young to set more limits on their activities. "Now we feel like we're in too deep," she said. "I'd tell preschool parents to decide ahead of time what they think is reasonable. We just sort of responded to what came along, and now it would be hard to ask the kids to give up something."

In other words, she is experiencing the snowball effect that results from trying to make life completely fair for her kids. After all, if one gets to play three sports, shouldn't they all? The wisest thing my mother ever told me when I would protest that something wasn't fair was this: "Life isn't fair." It's harsh, but it is true. If you believe it, you *don't* "have to let the others do" what their older siblings are doing. When you can let go of the burden of trying to make life "fair" in an unfair world, you are free to treat your children as individuals who might have different capacities and different needs.

Breathing Exercise

Write out the weekly schedule you and your family keep. Add up the hours you spend in the car. How many hours do your kids have to just "hang out" and play in an unstructured way? If you hear yourself saying that you want to give your kids an "opportunity," take the time to ask, "an opportunity for what?" Lay your schedule out in front of you and pray. Tell God about what kind of burden this schedule feels like. Ask God to show you what one or two small steps you might take to eliminate hurry from your life. What could you prune from your schedule? Ask yourself about each obligation, "What's the worst that might happen if I don't do this?"

Hurry Creeps In

Do you weigh the same as you did when you were in high school? Most Americans do not. I know I don't. If we even gain just one pound a year, we won't look the same at our tenth high school reunion as we did on graduation day.

But how did we get there? One French fry at a time. It's not as if you went to sleep weighing 120 and woke up tipping the scales at 140 the next day. Your metabolism changed, your eating habits changed, you had a kid or two, and after a few years, your body just didn't look like it did when you were eighteen.

Hurry is like that. It creeps up on you. You add another project at work, you say yes to one more committee at church, you agree to be room mom at school one more year. You join the neighborhood bowling league because it's "only once a month."

I know I've often said yes to things I don't have time for because I rationalize that it's not a daily obligation. One year I said yes to four things that were "only once a month" and realized that I had set myself up for a weekly obligation without even realizing it! No wonder I feel weary and burdened.

We live in a culture focused on doing. That's one reason so many of us wrestle with being a parent: time with our kids doesn't seem like we are producing anything. To ruthlessly eliminate hurry would make us feel "unproductive," which we're afraid is actually a sin. We'd also have to actually be a parent, to connect with our kids, and we're not sure we can do that well. We don't know how to measure our success there, so again, we feel unproductive, which is very uncomfortable.

But what if time that seems "unproductive" actually isn't? I mean time when we focus on simply being with God, or just being—couldn't that "produce" some things in our life, like peace and joy?

A lot of people say they want to simplify their lives. The hard part is getting started. The good news, though, is that you don't have to get it right all at once. Slowing down is a process, and taking one step at a time is the only way to engage in that process.

Eliminating hurry from your life will reduce your stress level and begin to open up some space for God in your life. It is the first step toward Sabbath Simplicity. Not only will it help you grow, but experts say that slowing down will also make your children healthier and more creative.

The Hurried Child

Part of the reason moms have "hurried woman" syndrome is because their children are also hurried. Our society pushes children to grow up too fast, says David Elkind in his book *The Hurried Child*. Hurry is not just about being overscheduled, although that's part of it. Pushing a two-year-old to read, allowing your six-year-old to dress like Britney Spears, letting your young children play violent video games—these are all things that hurry our children into growing up too fast, Elkind warns. He argues that children have been turned into "mini-achievers" and have not been allowed to just be kids. Through television, they are given graphic images of violence, sex, war, and other realities of our world that they are not emotionally equipped to deal with. As a result of being hurried, kids today are under enormous amounts of stress. Elkind points to childhood obesity and increased violence as results of this stress.

Do your children have time to do childlike things? Do you let them say yes to Jesus's invitation to simply rest? Our society is slowly losing track of what it even means to be a child. We want our children to be productive and efficient, even though developmentally, being creative and taking their time would be much more beneficial. We stress competence and competition in ways that are unhealthy. This manifests itself not only in sports but in academic pressures as well, even on very young children.

"While parents have traditionally taken pride in their offspring's achievements and have been concerned about their education, it is a unique characteristic of contemporary society that we burden preschoolers with the expectations and anxieties normally (if wrongly) visited upon high school seniors. Today, parents brag not only about the colleges and prep schools their children are enrolled in but also about which private kindergartens they attend."[1]

Elkind first took note of these problems in the late 1970s and early '80s. That means many of today's parents were hurried children themselves. They grew up doing too much, were pushed too hard, exposed to too much. Elkind harshly criticizes organized sports, especially for young children. "At the preschool age," he writes, "children will gain much more from their own spontaneous play than they will from any organized sport."[2]

Despite Elkind preaching this message for twenty years or more, young kids today are still in highly competitive, organized sports. They are pushed to grow up even faster now than they were ten years ago. Parents who grew up in Little League and travel soccer don't know anything different, so what they are doing to their own children feels normal. That makes it even harder to go against the grain.

Many adults who overschedule their kids seem unaware that their children don't have time to "just play." Ironically, the children are busy "playing" sports, but to them it doesn't feel like play. Why? There are many reasons, including the fact that many kids are pushed into activities that reflect their parents' interests and drive for success more than their own. But mostly, organized sports are too structured. To most young kids, extreme structure and fun are polar opposites.

I'm not saying kids don't need some structure and limits, because I know they do need them. But kids on a team run by adults (as opposed to those just playing tag or kickball in the backyard) miss out on some things: the chance to learn to negotiate with other kids about who is on what team and who plays each position. Often, backyard games include rules or roles that the kids make up as they go along, which teaches them to think on their feet and use their imagination.

But it is the structure of sports or other "classes" that appeals to parents. The kids are not wasting time; they are being productive, learning a skill, working toward a goal. In our culture, these things are highly valued. Why? Productivity is important for machines, but is it that important for children? Can creativity and productivity be nurtured simultaneously? Is competency at an early age the most important thing we should cultivate in our children?

Some kids enjoy sports, but often sports create stress. Think about it. Imagine you are five. "This is a soccer ball," the coach says. "You kick it. I know you've never played this game, but we expect you to do it really well. The idea is to kick the ball into the goal. You're not just kicking it around for fun. You're trying to win. We're going to line you up in two teams on a field, and we're going to have some adults in canvas folding chairs sit on the sidelines. They're going to scream at you while you try to kick the ball toward the goal. The other kids will try to kick it, and likely, they will be able to kick it away from you. Then the adults will scream even more. They'll all be yelling different things, so you won't be able to understand what they are saying. You can pretty much bet that your parents will be telling you to do one thing while I, your coach, will be telling you another."

I doubt a coach would actually tell our kids these things. Even peewee soccer has its spin doctors. "Isn't this fun?" we say, telling more than asking. I saw a newspaper article recently in which several children were quoted as saying that they wouldn't play soccer at all if it weren't for the high-calorie nutritionally bereft treats given out after the game. That's right: it's not our yelling that motivates our kids, it's the promise of a juice box and a bag of Cheetos.

I've been one of those screaming adults, and it wasn't much fun for me either. I'd come home with an angry child and a sore throat. Through painful experiences for myself and my children, I've learned a lot about keeping quiet on the sidelines of my kids' sporting events. But it does not surprise me when I overhear children saying, "I don't want to go to soccer practice right now, Mom—I'm playing." That is, playing at some game of the child's own devising, playing at something that does not involve adults telling the child what to do and how to do it.

I am not opposed to organized sports. My daughter is on a soccer team. But she's not on two different soccer teams, a baseball team, and the swim team as well. Her schedule purposely includes several days a week where she has no lessons, no obligations (other than school and homework). She has time to read and to just listen to music in her room or play with a friend. I create space in our calendar for these types of days, because I have come to realize that my kids also need time for unstructured activities where no adult is directing them. Why? Because it's important for them developmentally. If kids have adults directing them 24-7, they don't know how to direct themselves. That's why so many kids say to their parents, "I'm bored!"

When Jesus said we need to come to him as a little child, he wasn't thinking of today's overscheduled, hurried kids. He was thinking of someone who knows how to just be, how to take life as it comes and notice the wonder in ordinary things. Are you cultivating those character qualities in your children? Ironically, the way to cultivate such things is to step back and not hover, plan, or schedule. Provide a safe environment and appropriate supervision but not too many directions.

For example, on a warm day, give a toddler a couple of small buckets of water and several small plastic cups. Put him in the backyard, sit in a lawn chair nearby, and watch what happens. Without any instructions, the child will probably dump at least one bucket on himself, but he will enjoy scooping water from one bucket to the other with the cups. He may learn some things, and he may get a little messy, but mostly he'll have fun.

Breathing Exercise

Do you and your children have time to simply play? Do you relax with them, or give them time to just "hang out"? What might be some of the benefits of having such time? How might time to daydream and read affect your child's spiritual life? How might allowing this kind of thing affect your ability to trust, to not have to control?

Setting a Sustainable Pace

The pace of your kids' lives is the pace of *your* life. You can't slow yourself down without slowing them down. You can't simplify your life without simplifying their lives, especially if they don't yet drive themselves and they can't walk to soccer practice.

You may feel pressured to sign your children up for baby swim classes, preschool language classes, and, by the time they are four or five, competitive sports leagues.

But do you give them time to play?

Not Nintendo. Not Little League. Just play. Kids who are playing are not on a schedule, so they move from one activity to the next and back again without anyone telling them to do so. Do your kids have time to play? Time to climb trees, draw with sidewalk chalk, or dig for worms in the backyard? Time to play make-believe or dress-up, ride bikes or jump rope, play in a sandbox or run through a sprinkler? Or are they (and you) too busy?

My kitchen window looks out on my backyard, and I love seeing my son out there, swinging on the swing, singing and talking to himself about everything and nothing. He is building neuron connections by the minute, sorting out his thoughts to the rhythm of the swing, without any help from me.

The hard part about trying to live this way is, he's often on the swing set by himself. Which is okay, sometimes. But when he'd like to socialize, it's not always possible, because everyone else is at soccer practice (or baseball or Tae Kwon Do, or wherever).

Dr. Elkind has studied and written about this problem since *The Hurried Child* was first published in 1981. In the introduction to the third edition (2001), he notes: "After talking with parents all over the country, I have found that many are really trying very hard not to hurry their children, but feel forced into it because of what other parents are doing, namely, enrolling their children in organized sports and other programs. This problem is particularly pernicious for the parents of young children. If parents do not enroll their children in these programs, their children are left without playmates."[3]

I've experienced this problem firsthand. One summer I chose to let my kids simply play and not have structured activities. They didn't go to camp or take swimming lessons. We had a great time and spent a lot of time together. We let go of our normal structured life for a couple of months. My kids really enjoyed having a lot of free time, but they often had trouble finding someone to play with because all their friends seemed to be at camp for much of the time.

The upside for our family was that my children played with each other and, I think, grew closer as a result. They had to get along, because there was no one else to play with. They also learned to be comfortable being alone, which very few people have the opportunity to learn.

I was encouraged by Dr. Elkind's words: "You can use the lack of playmates as an opportunity for your children to learn to be comfortable on their own, to discover their inner resources of imagination and creativity."[4]

If you have very young children, now is the time to let them play. Turn off the television, unplug the video games, and get outside and play!

I first read Elkind's book when my children were still in diapers, and I decided that I wanted my kids to have plenty of time to simply be, to play, to read, or draw, or daydream. So at our house, we have that built into our schedule. I didn't sign them up for reading classes or classes on developing their imagination. I read to them a lot but also let them sit and look at books, draw, or play with blocks. We limit television and computer time; we don't have cable television or a video game player of any kind. We spend a lot of time playing outside, digging in the garden, playing in sand, noticing bugs or other creatures.

As my kids reached the age where many of their friends were beginning to be involved in activities, I set this rule: you may do one sport at a time and one artistic endeavor. You don't have to do anything if you don't want to. My kids did Kindermusik, a program I strongly admire because it is play-oriented rather than accomplishment-oriented. But that was it when they were small. Eventually, my daughter chose soccer as her sport, and after graduating from

Kindermusik, went on to take piano, which she absolutely loves.

My son has tried a variety of sports (one at a time!!!). He enjoyed Kindermusik but struggled with piano. I knew that he often spent his free time drawing pictures, so I asked if he'd prefer to take a drawing class instead. He loves doing something that he's better at than his older sister, and we're amazed as we watch his skills develop.

Still, holding to my ideals of an unhurried life isn't easy. When we received a flyer in the mail about tryouts for the children's choir at our church, I showed it to Melanie, who was eight at the time. I imagined her singing at church and from there, going on to win on *American Idol*. I ignored the fact that rehearsals and performances could sometimes result in her needing to be at church three nights in one week. I admit, I liked envisioning my little girl up there on stage. I tried to sell her on joining the group, knowing she's very musical and enjoys performing. She burst my bubble rather quickly by simply echoing the words I'd been telling her for several years. "Mom, I don't want to be that busy," she told me. "Besides, you told us we should only do one sport and one art. I'm not giving up piano to do choir."

I realized that my desire for her to be in the choir was not about her. It was about me. I envisioned myself basking in the glow of her accomplishments. I don't like to admit this, but at the moment, it was true. I'm thankful that in my saner moments, I have taught her to keep things simple and be very clear about setting boundaries.

Since I'd been consistent about the limits, she believed in them. They're really there. Choir might have been fun, but it wasn't worth giving up piano, something she really enjoys.

Breathing Exercise

Are your kids hurried? If they are very young, have you given any thought to how you will respond to "opportunities" when they come up in the future? Do you feel pressure to hurry your kids?

Eliminating Hurry

So how can we, as Dallas Willard has advised, "ruthlessly eliminate hurry" from our lives?

The problem is, if you've gotten in the habit of doing too much, you can't eliminate hurry in a hurry. You're going to have to approach change deliberately but slowly.

You can't drop everything. You've still got to drive the car pool; arrange the playdates; give time, attention, food, and clean-up services to your children; and get your own work done (paid or unpaid, at home or outside the home). But there is a way to prune your schedule and a way to approach the remaining things that will allow you to connect deeply with God, which in turn will allow you to breathe.

As I said before, I have been on my own journey toward a simpler, less hurried life for several years. Throughout this book I will share some practical steps that have helped me in that journey, even though I am far from figuring everything out. The Breathing Exercises will give you the opportunity to try them out.

I still find myself getting stressed, especially during the holidays or when I'm on deadline with a big project. I long to simplify, and I even start to do so, but then things somehow spin out of control. I feel like I'm on the teacup ride at Disney World. At first, I'm turning the wheel and setting the pace. The spinning is fun and somehow contained. But then the momentum builds, and even if I let go of the wheel in the center of the teacup, we continue to spin faster and faster. I feel a little sick.

This year I wanted a peaceful Advent. I went on a retreat at the beginning of December to focus on the true meaning of the season. I thought I was fairly organized. I kept our gift lists for the kids short, and my husband and I agreed that we didn't want more stuff, we wanted time together; so rather than buying expensive and needless gifts for one another, we'd plan to have a night out together as our "gift" to one another.

Despite my intentions in November, I found myself snapping at people by mid-December. "You just don't understand," I told my husband as I made cookie dough one night at 11:00. "I do all the shopping, baking, planning, wrapping, shipping. I am making Christmas happen around here."

A few times, I was vaguely aware of the irony of my declaration that I was "making Christmas happen." Um, well, not exactly. But part of my busyness is really self-deception. I am thinking that Christmas literally would not happen if I didn't keep buying and baking, organizing and obsessing. Original sin, according to the Bible, occurred when Adam and Eve thought they could be like God. Rather than celebrate Advent, rather than reflect on the miracle of Christ's incarnation, I am becoming the poster child for original sin. I am trying to play God. I *think* I am making the world spin. The problem with spinning, as I know from riding the teacup ride, is that sometimes the momentum takes you to a place you don't want to go.

Christmas would have happened with or without my efforts, but as it was, I dropped the ball on a few things, including one teacher's gift I forgot to send on the last day of school. Every year I say I'm going to take it slow, enjoy the season, appreciate the true meaning of Christmas. It doesn't always happen.

I have moments when I do slow down. This year, we lit Advent candles on Sundays and talked with the kids about the significance of this ritual. That was great. I want to learn more about things like this. But there were also moments when I thought, *This is crazy*. I also got a bit resentful of my husband, who sat on the couch as I wrapped another pile of presents I had purchased from six different stores and told me I ought to relax. Not a good thing to say to a woman with scissors in her hand.

Christmas did happen at our house, and now, in January, I have what I call my post-Christmas stress disorder head cold. I think sometimes I hurry and try to do too much because I really do think that the world will stop if I get off the magic treadmill that keeps it going. The trouble with the rat race, as they say, is that even if you win, you're still a rat.

Take a Deep Breath

We're all busy, for a variety of reasons. We often feel stressed and hurried. What can we do about it?

Think about this: When you get really stressed, what do you say to yourself? When your two-year-old throws himself on the floor as he has yet another tantrum, what do you do? When you walk into the house after carpooling for what feels like hours, the kids are crabby, and you're trying to get groceries unpacked and dinner on the table, and you think you might scream, what do you tell yourself? I often say, even out loud sometimes, "Okay, take a deep breath." Reminding myself to breathe slowly and deeply calms me down, at least for a moment.

When my daughter was that magical age of almost two, she used to get easily frustrated. I'm sure that never happens to your kids, but mine would start to mutter and sputter and almost hyperventilate if things got complicated (putting on her shoes was something that could get complicated). "Eehh, ehhh, ehhh . . ." she'd say, her voice rising in pitch and volume with each exhaled noise, and I knew we were on our way down Tantrum Road.

So I'd tell her, "Melanie, take a deep breath; breathe like this," and then I'd demonstrate a slow, cleansing breath, in through the nose, out through the mouth.

One day, *I* was the one about to have a tantrum, frustrated by some situation I can't even recall now, but I think it may have involved trying to get her to do something I wanted (like put her shoes on). When I began to fume, my darling little one looked at me and said, "Mama, take a deep breath, like this," and proceeded to show me several slow breaths in animated exaggeration. Thankfully, I was not too far down Tantrum Road myself, so I was able to laugh.

I taught my daughter, and she also reminded me, but we all know it instinctively: sometimes, all we need is to slow down and provide our brains with a little oxygen.

But there is more to it than just that.

The Bible says that when God created man, he formed him from dust, then "breathed into his nostrils the breath of life, and man became a living being" (Gen. 2:7). There was more than respiration involved here. In addition to getting man's lungs working, there is another, more symbolic layer of meaning in the text. God was giving man a soul, a spirit.

And when the resurrected Jesus appeared to his disciples, the Bible says that "he breathed on them and said, 'Receive the Holy Spirit'" (John 20:22). Again, the symbolism is rich. What God did to Adam—breathing life into him and a spirit into him—Christ is doing for his people, who would become the church: breathing its initial life into it and filling it with his Spirit.

In both Greek and Hebrew, the ancient original languages of the Bible, we often see two words for this. In the Old Testament Hebrew, the word was *ruach*. In the New Testament Greek, it was *pneuma*. Both can be translated "spirit" or "breath" or sometimes even "power."

The language was no accident. God is not some distant, far-off deity. His Spirit is as close as the air you breathe. Every breath you take can be a reminder that God is with you.

Even in our language, the words *breath* and *spirit* are connected. Saying something such as, "It took my breath away," doesn't mean we stopped breathing. It means our spirit was deeply affected. We felt awe, amazement, even fear. We had a strong reaction, deep in our being.

So the next time you hear yourself saying, "Take a deep breath," consider that you are really telling yourself to connect with God, to pray. Your brain may need oxygen, but just as much, your soul needs a calming and loving presence.

Prayer is not just rattling off a list of needs and wants at God. Prayer is simply being with God. Being quiet, telling him what's going on with you, listening for his response. Sometimes it's simply saying, "Lord, you know I didn't get enough sleep last night and this child is driving me crazy. Help me to be patient. I need your peace in my heart and in my words." Sometimes all we can say is "Help!" but God understands.

It's easy to trivialize prayer, and we don't appreciate when well-meaning people tell us to "just pray about it." I usually assume that someone who says this doesn't understand my situation, and in that case, "Just pray" sounds like a pat answer.

It's only a pat answer if I let it be. I know I have sometimes confused prayer with a monologue directed at God. So if I pray about my difficulties or stress, it's kind of like filing a complaint with him. This only helps sometimes. But lately I've discovered another kind of prayer that works much better.

It involves breathing, and listening, and focusing on God, rather than on myself. This type of prayer is incredibly calming because it allows me to connect with God, even when I'm feeling stressed out.

The only way you will remember to pray this way when you are under stress is to practice it when you are not. So let's do that right now.

Breathing Exercise

Sit still, wherever you are at this moment. Take a deep breath, in through your nose, then blowing out slowly and fully through your mouth. Do this several times. Relax your body, but sit upright (it's not nap time!). As you breathe in, breathe deeply enough that your stomach (not your chest) goes out a bit, then as you breathe out, pull your stomach muscles in to push the air out. Let go of distractions and worries as you breathe out. You are not trying to empty your mind entirely but rather fill it with simple awareness of God. Think about your inhaling breath as breathing in God's presence. Allow yourself to be in the moment, not thinking about your to-do list or the things you've already done or felt today. Be present. You may want to say a single-word prayer: "Jesus" or "Father." At this point, you are not asking for anything except to be fully present in this moment and to be aware of God's presence.

The first time you try this exercise, you may or may not feel God's presence. If you think only that you want to be in the present moment, you will begin to calm down. Even if you aren't aware of God, that doesn't mean he's not there.

God is with you, always, whether you are aware of it or not. That's why hurry is so damaging. If you rush past something, you don't always see it. Hurry keeps you from seeing God all around. Breathing slowly, if you continue to practice it, will help you to experience God in a new way.

This exercise is about trust: Trust that if you sit still and ask God to make you aware of his presence, he will do so. Trust that some things are true even if you don't see them immediately.

If we are going to slow down, we need to replace our craziness, not with nothing but with meaningful things that help us to focus, help us to breathe. Our longing for simplicity begs the question, what exactly is simplicity and where do I find it?

part two

the challenge

Take my yoke upon you
and learn from me

3

scattered

Whose approval am I seeking?

Most people who knew Laura admired her. She seemed to always have time for others, even though she and her three young children kept very busy. She homeschooled her kids, her house always looked great, and she volunteered a lot of her time at church. She seemed to be able to get a lot done while staying calm and cool. Anytime someone needed a shoulder to cry on, Laura was there. Anytime there was a need for someone to help out at church, Laura was there.

Like many of us, Laura was a giver. She had been a Christian her whole life, and many people looked to her to meet their needs for advice, spiritual leadership, friendship, even help in parenting (or at least babysitting!).

Also like many of us, Laura had trouble saying no. She felt she ought to help others if she could, and as a result, she helped even if she really had too many other commitments.

In addition to helping others whenever they asked, she threw herself into her homeschooling tasks. She put the kids in extracurricular classes and activities to "enrich their experience."

She was involved in several ministries at her church, serving on various teams and committees, wherever there was a need.

She seemed to be the epitome of unselfishness—always doing for others. Looking back, Laura says, no one really knew the anger and resentment that bubbled below the surface. "I wanted to give people the perception that I was available," she says. "I said yes mostly to validate my importance." In other words, she was bearing burdens she was never meant to bear. And doing it because she thought it would please God.

Laura was adept at keeping a calm appearance, when in reality, she was full of emotions she didn't know how to process or even feel.

If we are honest about our busyness, we'll admit that we're a lot like Laura: saying yes to every request because of what it does for our ego or to avoid feeling guilty, but feeling resentment about the way other people's needs crowd our schedules and drain our energy. We look like we've got it all together, but inside, we're scattered. Like Laura, many of us wrestle with our desire for significance, and we're scared that if we don't keep other people happy, we won't be important.

Laura's frustration with her own inability to set boundaries, however, was just the tip of the iceberg. Her husband, Don, was a busy executive in a stressful job, and his stress level kept increasing. In addition to his responsibilities at work, he also said yes when asked to become an elder at their church. His stress level obviously affected his family, but Laura, always wanting to be supportive and helpful, didn't complain. In fact, she tried to keep herself as busy as he was.

"I'd look at my husband's life and think, if I'm busy, I'm just as important as him," she says. "So people would call and ask if they could come over, or if I could watch their kids—again!—and I'd of course say yes, when I wanted to say no. But then it would build into resentment."

Because Don was so busy and stressed, "I felt like I had to work extra hard at home to make sure things were smooth. He even told me once he had no reserves. I decided I needed to make sure everything at home was perfect so that he didn't have to handle anything at home."

When she'd spend a few minutes before bed praying and reviewing her day, "I'd be miserable," she says. "But I was addicted to having a lot of plates spinning. If I had a day with nothing to do, I'd find something to do. I was hurried inside. I'd knowingly double-book myself, saying yes to two different commitments that I knew were at the same time. Then I'd call and cancel one of the things at the last minute. Somehow that seemed better than saying no in the first place. I wanted to create the impression that I had plenty of available space. I especially wanted to say yes if I was asked to do something at church. I was afraid if I said no, people would stop asking."

Laura wanted to make sure everyone thought she was doing a good job. She remembers feeling fearful when her youngest child got to the age when he no longer took naps, because she would not have an excuse to be home during the afternoon. Just choosing to be home during the afternoon and saying no to invitations at that time never seemed like an option, she says. Ironically, she seemed to forget that when she canceled things at the last minute, she was coming up with made-up excuses. Just saying, "No, I would prefer to just have a day at home, so I can't come and help out," were words she simply couldn't bring herself to say. If someone needed her time, she felt obligated to give it, unless she had what she felt was a valid, "unselfish" excuse. She also felt obligated to smile and act as if everything was wonderful, even if she felt frustrated.

"I worked hard at keeping up appearances," she says. "I was always focused on the task. But I wasn't focused on the person I was with, or God, or myself. When I was with someone, I was thinking about what I had to do next. I had a hard time being present with people. But my friends would never know that. Even my family thought I was fine. I looked calm on the outside. Sometimes that was true of what was inside me, but sometimes it wasn't. It would sometimes keep me up at night."

Laura was tired. She knew that at times her resentment would seep out as anger when she would yell at her family. She wanted to change. "I began to ask myself: Who do I want to be with? What do I need? Could I have relationships where I was the receiver instead of the giver?"

She talked with a spiritual mentor about this and began to notice patterns in her behavior. But there is a big difference between seeing a pattern and having the courage to change. She still found she had trouble being honest with her friends. But just being open to discussing the truth with her mentor began a slow (and sometimes painful) journey that took her from being scattered to being focused. She didn't call it that, but she was moving toward Sabbath Simplicity by changing her focus from what others wanted her to do to what God wanted her to be.

The First Step

In 1998, Laura decided to try running a marathon. She had always enjoyed running for exercise, but until she started training for the marathon, her longest run had been about eight miles. It was the first time in a long time she'd done something for herself rather than for other people.

"When you are training for a marathon, the training regimen requires that you do certain things and you not do other things," she says. "You don't eat a big bowl of ice cream the night before a ten-mile training run. You say yes and no to certain things for a reason. I became really focused on achieving the goal of finishing the marathon. I'm an experiential learner, so as I trained for it, there was a lot of learning for me, not just about running but about life."

Laura carefully followed a regimen that gradually increased her endurance. But she found it interesting that the schedule didn't simply add a few blocks of running each day. Rather, it included days of shorter runs, days of longer runs, and days of prescribed rest. It's not that running was optional on those days. Resting was required and was the most helpful thing she could do if she hoped to achieve the goal of completing the twenty-six-mile race. The resting days were just as important as the running days.

The training schedule became a model for the need she had in her life for finding time to rest. The Christian life is a marathon, not a sprint. In order to finish the race, you have to follow a training schedule that includes not just days of running but also times of rest.

When she ran and completed the marathon, Laura felt much more than a sense of accomplishment. God had met her in the process. "A big 'aha' for me was that if I can live my life focused on this goal, I could live my life focused on God," she says. "Instead of just lying in bed wishing it were different, I began to realize there were things I could do to change."

During her training, she was reading the book of Hebrews, especially chapters 11 and 12. Her reflection on the Scriptures reinforced what she was learning as a result of her physical training. After the marathon, she got a license plate for her car that says "HBRWS 12 1" to remind her of the verse that inspired her during that time: "Therefore, since we are surrounded by such a great cloud of witnesses, let us throw off everything that hinders and the sin that so easily entangles, and let us run with perseverance the race marked out for us" (Heb. 12:1).

Inspired by her learning, Laura began the long process of throwing off the things that hindered her from, as the next verse in Hebrews 12 says, fixing her eyes on Jesus. She began to be more deliberate about what she said yes to and what she said no to. She began to realize that it was okay to disappoint people sometimes. She began to incorporate spiritual practices into her life, such as silence, as she would turn off the radio in the car or at home.

She continues to look for ways to incorporate silence into her days. "Silence takes work," she says. "Rather than just fill up the space with noise, I sit and just be still. I try to figure out what I'm feeling at that moment, and why. That's hard."

On the advice of her spiritual mentor, she started daring to say no to pleasing people and yes to pleasing God.

Despite these learnings, Laura was still doing a lot. She continued to homeschool her children and kept them involved in plenty of outside activities. She was still very involved at church, as were her children and husband. But the next step in their family's journey toward simplicity was a doozy.

A Painful Lesson

Laura was beginning to slow the pace of her life somewhat, but her husband, Don, was not. He was under tremendous pressure at work, often working eighty hours or more a week. He started feeling sick. He noticed strange symptoms, including vertigo, fatigue, even changes in the texture of his leg muscles. Once he got sick on an airplane and had to be taken off the plane. He searched medical websites on the Internet, wondering if he had multiple sclerosis or some other disease. But he kept working hard, not making a connection between the pace of his life and the physical symptoms he was experiencing.

One day Don was at the health club, jogging on the treadmill, when he collapsed. The paramedics rushed to the scene, checked him out, but could find nothing wrong.

Later, his doctor told him he was stressed out and advised him to relax. "That was not too helpful for us," Laura noted. Don didn't know how to relax. And was stress causing the other symptoms? He kept trying to figure out what was wrong.

Eventually, Don found help from a chiropractor/naturopath who told him that the stress was causing his adrenal system to not function properly. His work, though most of it was done at a desk or in a board room, was taking a toll on his body.

The pace and stress of his life had kept him running on adrenaline almost all the time.

"Our bodies have adrenaline because we need it for certain situations," Laura says. "Like if you are being chased through the woods by a bear, adrenalin helps you run away. But a lot of people live their lives as if they were being chased by a bear every day."

Living in "hyped-up" mode all the time didn't give Don's body or mind time to rest and recover. Because of this, the naturopath told him, his physical and emotional reserves were completely depleted. He was mentally, physically, and emotionally exhausted and desperately needed to stop living every moment as if he were being chased by a bear.

Don took a leave of absence from work to recover. He began reevaluating his schedule and commitments and eventually changed jobs.

"The pain of Don getting sick caused me to ask myself some hard questions," Laura says. "My high-powered, achieving, strong husband was suddenly needy and sad. And if he had decided during that time not to be an elder, well, then, I wouldn't be an elder's wife anymore. And I had to think about why that was important to me. I found myself asking, 'What are the voices that drive me?' I had to let go of a lot of stuff, a lot of image management. When pain entered my home, I didn't know what to do with it, because I was so fragmented and was juggling so many things."

Don's illness changed the family's priorities too. "We went from saying, 'Gee, we really need to say no to some things,' to 'Why are we saying yes to things?'"

The difference is subtle but important. Just feeling that you ought to slow down is not the same as actually doing it. Wishing you could live differently is not enough to make it happen. Simplifying means really examining your motivation for keeping busy and hurried. Just vaguely saying you "should" or "ought to" do something won't make life simpler.

Looking at why she did the things she did was Laura's next step. It required deep introspection and self-examination. She needed to open up space to listen to Jesus, to fully respond to his invitation to learn from him what the easy yoke was really about.

"Don's crash led to both of us looking at what we were carrying and if what we were carrying was even necessary," Laura says. "If people don't get the simplicity thing right, not only will their emotional and spiritual world be impacted, but their physical world will as well."

Don's being unwell for several months caused Laura to rethink a lot of what she was doing and to make some major changes in the pace of her life.

"I realized that who I was had been shaped by who I thought people wanted me to be," Laura admits. "Now, as a family, we ask, 'Is saying yes to this going to make us more loving? Is it going to enrich our lives or clutter them?'"

One key to her commitment to simplicity was incorporating a Sabbath into her week. "Sunday is a day that I spend doing things that re-create me," she says. "I don't do laundry. I try to just read or be outside. We used to always stop at the grocery store on the way home from church. I hated that. But Don liked to do it. So I said, drop me off at home first."

To let go of doing something just because someone else wanted to do it was a huge step for Laura. She didn't force the issue, but she invited her family into a day of rest.

"Don would pull out his laptop on a Sunday afternoon to do some work," she says. "I'd just look at him and say, 'You really need a day of rest.'" But she didn't push it. For her, it was a big enough step just to make her own decisions and to begin to take care of herself. These days, her family tends to join her in the weekly day of rest.

Attending to the stirrings in her soul is one way for her to learn from Jesus. It's helping Laura become more peaceful and joyful and also more honest. When she takes time to learn and understand what's going on in her mind and heart, she's better able to express those thoughts and feelings to others, instead of simply reacting with what she thinks they want to hear.

Breathing Exercise

What circumstances in your life is God using to guide you toward dealing with some of the deeper issues of life? For Laura and Don, it took a crash to inspire them to change. What will it take for you? Do you ever give yourself the time to notice or attend to the stirrings in your soul? How much are you, as Laura says she was, "shaped by who I thought people wanted me to be"? What would happen if you were shaped instead by God's love for you and his calling on your life?

Deeper Still

Laura continued to create space for God by being careful to say no to things that didn't enrich her life. She also sought to create space for God by incorporating spiritual practices that kept her focused on him. She continued to respond to Jesus's invitation into a life-giving way of life, to learn from him.

"Ever since I can remember, I would get these leadings," she said. "God would tell me to do something for someone. I loved to do that. Maybe leave them a gift, or send them a note, do something nice for them."

She still does those things, but lately, "I've been practicing secrecy. Which I can't tell you too much about, or it won't be a secret," she said, smiling. "If I get some sort of leading, I'll do it, but I won't tell anyone. It really tests what drives me: God's approval or other people's."

She's continued to deepen her practice of Sabbath, spending one day a week doing things that she enjoys and refusing to do things like checking email, doing laundry, or returning phone calls if she thinks the conversation will drain her in any way.

Laura was learning a lot and had listened to God's direction and cut back on her commitments at church dramatically.

Before Don's illness, however, she had made a commitment to teach at a women's retreat. A team of teachers was each taking a different spiritual practice as their topic. Laura had said yes to teaching on "Simplicity." Little did she know how much God was going to teach her by allowing her to teach.

"It was hard, because I thought I was further along in my journey than I actually was," she said. "I didn't really want to go and teach, but God wanted me to. I had some things to learn. Like, for instance, the painful things in my life at that time with Don's illness made me want to self-medicate by buying things. But then I had to prepare to teach about how we handle our stuff. It forced me to deal with how far I had to go on that issue."

Teaching on simplicity brought her face-to-face with the fact "that I often overscheduled the kids and me to avoid pain. I didn't have time to figure out what to do with the pain. I was raised to just smile my way through it. So I tried to find some way to ease the pain. But teaching others about simplicity showed me I was not as far as I thought I was."

Laura realized that she could not ignore these revelations. She dropped out of all commitments at church after the retreat and spent several months working with a counselor and spending large chunks of time reflecting and praying. She continued to homeschool her children, but she began to say no to most other requests for her time or energy.

On the advice of her naturopath doctor, she and her family also began to practice deep, slow breathing as a way to cope with stress and to slow themselves down.

Learning to breathe became another picture of the steps she was taking with her schedule and her life, Laura says.

"I wanted to be the same person all the time," she says, rather than being what she thought others wanted her to be, or trying to be like people she admired. Like most of us, she often admired people who were different than she was. She was afraid they might not accept the real her, so she felt she ought to pretend to be like them.

"Today, I can embrace the fact that I like to walk barefoot in the grass, that I like to make things," she says. "It's kind of a funny thing, but here's one thing I did. My daughter wanted to have an Indian dress to play dress-up in. I had thought about making it for her, because I like doing that kind of thing, but I never had time. Or I never made time, because it didn't seem like something I 'ought' to do. Well, when I took some time to slow my life down, I discovered I had time, so I made her this Indian dress, with fringe and beads and all. She loved it. And I realized that making an Indian dress for my daughter is just as important in God's eyes as teaching at a retreat or leading an important ministry at church. There's just this freedom in being myself that I discovered. And that's really the beauty of simplicity."

Breathing Exercise

Sit and take several deep, slow breaths. What is your response to Laura's story? What desires or fears did it stir within you? Breathe slowly and deeply and let your response surface from your heart. When faced with choices about how to spend your time, do you tend to say, "Gee, I really need to say no to some things," or "Why am I saying yes to things?" What would happen if you actually examined your motives for saying yes? What would happen if you said no to some things in order to say yes to focusing on your relationship with God?

Double Trouble

Do you focus on what God wants you to do or on what would best maintain your image? This may not be about wearing the right clothes or having a fancy home. Many of us say we couldn't care less about the material stuff but are very dedicated to making sure we maintain our image as a "deeply spiritual person" or a "dedicated church member" or a "super parent." If we are honest about whether our focus is on God or on image management, we may say, well, both. I want to please God and show him my love, but I also want to get other people to like me. These two goals are not always mutually exclusive; that is, some things we do might accomplish both. For example, making dinner for your neighbor who just had a baby is something that would please God and will probably cause her to appreciate you. But why are you doing it? Where is your focus? If you focus on God, the rest of the things you need will fall into place.

The opposite of simplicity is not complexity but duplicity. Duplicity means we are divided—we have a split personality. We don't have a singular focus but rather multiple focuses, which create a feeling of being pulled in a thousand directions.

Sometimes we have our faith on one hand, our real life on the other, and they never come together. We act one way when we are with our Christian friends but another way at work or with the neighbors. We maybe have our "church face" that pretends everything is great, but it's hiding who we really are or what is happening in our lives. We miss out on the spiritual significance of parenting, of our jobs, of anything we don't label as "Christian" or "religious." We're what the Bible calls "double-minded," or duplicitous.

The Bible says that when we let go of our own agenda and seek after God, everything else falls into place. "Seek first his kingdom and his righteousness, and all these things will be given to you as well" (Matt. 6:33). That doesn't mean everything becomes easy. It simply means that God will be with us in all things, and he will take care of us. Sabbath Simplicity means putting God in his rightful place, in the center of our focus, in charge of our hearts, and resting in that.

For Laura and Don, there was no question that they loved God. They served him, they taught their children about him, they had an intimate relationship with him. They were also extremely competent, which can be dangerous if you don't take a rest, if you don't say no once in a while. Seeking after God doesn't necessarily mean running yourself ragged on his behalf.

So how do we seek God? The Bible tells us: "Submit yourselves, then, to God. Resist the devil, and he will flee from you. Come near to God and he will come near to you. Wash your hands, you sinners, and purify your hearts, you double-minded" (James 4:7–8).

I want to "come near to God," but how? James uses strong language, but he's helpful. He explains that we need to be continually weeding out sin and looking at our hearts. Is your heart divided or pure? Something pure is not a mixture of things. Pure gold, for example, is not mixed with other metals. It is just gold and nothing else. A pure heart is focused on Christ. It is a heart transformed by Christ and motivated by him alone. A pure heart does not have mixed motives.

Purity of heart is not accomplished the minute we start our relationship with Jesus. But the process begins there. The good news is that God longs to help us in our journey toward single-mindedness. God promises in the Bible, "I will give you a new heart and put a new spirit in you; I will remove from you your heart of stone and give you a heart of flesh" (Ezek. 36:26).

When God's Spirit moves in, Ezekiel says, you get a whole new heart. It's like Extreme Makeover, Heart Edition. Move toward God, James tells us, and he'll move toward you. He loves to answer the prayer, "Create in me a pure heart, O God" (Ps. 51:10).

How does God do that—create a pure heart? Washing your hands and cleaning your house are things that happen regularly—at least the washing of hands! Likewise, purifying our hearts is a process. But be encouraged: if you have given your heart to Christ, it is good. He is making all things new, and you have a good heart because of him.

But coming to know this is also a process, and not an easy one. Simplicity has a complexity to it. So the question is not, "Is my life complex?" Of course it is. Even keeping things simple requires decisions and strategies in today's society. The question is, "Is my heart divided (double-minded) or am I simply focused on Christ?"

We do not focus on Christ accidentally. We need to be intentional about it, or we will become scattered and distracted. We may work very hard, but that's not necessarily how to improve our focus.

Breathing Exercise

Sit and breathe for a moment. Think about slowing down. Invite Jesus to be with you. Take all the time you need to settle your spirit. Then ask, "Am I double-minded? Is my heart divided?" Listen to what God reveals to you. What worries, concerns, goals vie for your heart? What do you believe about your heart? Is it good?

The Trouble with Multitasking

As a mom, many things seem to clamor for my attention. It's hard to decide which voice I should listen to.

I am very good at multitasking. I can feed the kids dinner, quiz them on their spelling words, and drive them to soccer practice—all at the same time! I never just talk on the phone: I clean the kitchen, drive to the store, sometimes even walk the dog while returning phone calls or scheduling appointments.

I've noticed that moms with more children than I have get increasingly more adept at this, in direct proportion to the number of children they have.

The trouble with multitasking is that while we are able to get things done, we're not able to notice all the details of what we're doing. We miss moments. We are not fully present. It's like trying to have conversations with three people at once. We hear all of them, but we don't fully listen to any of them.

When we are focused on Christ, when our eyes are solely on him, we are able to notice him everywhere. He's integrated into our lives.

When I'm focused on Christ, I still might have to do some tasks. But it changes my perspective on those tasks. With my eyes on Christ, I can change a diaper as an act of service. It can be a reminder that Jesus has taken the stain of sin from my heart and made me clean again.

When I'm looking at Jesus, I can kiss away the tears of my toddler and comfort her the way Jesus comforts me. I can notice that he is present and remind myself to be fully present with my children.

When my eyes are on Jesus, any time I'm on my knees I'm reminded to pray, even if I'm on my knees playing Legos or Barbies.

If I have an opportunity at the playground to stand around with other moms and gossip about a neighbor, can I picture Jesus standing in our circle near the swings, listening to the conversation? What do I choose to say or not say? He is there, whether I choose to see him or not.

Fear Factor

What keeps us from simplicity, from a pure heart with a focus on Christ? I believe the main barrier to simplicity is the fear that threatens our hearts.

The Bible says, "Fear not, for I have redeemed you; I have called you by name; you are mine" (Isa. 43:1). Often, our lives are duplicitous because of fear.

We live in a world that gives us plenty of opportunities for fear. After the attacks of September 11, 2001, many Americans lived with an uneasiness and fear that we couldn't even put our finger on. I remember for months after that day, any time I saw a plane (and living close to Chicago's O'Hare Airport, I see a lot of planes), my mind would flash back to the images that replayed over and over that day on the television screen. I felt afraid. If I saw a plane that appeared to be flying lower than normal, it made me nervous.

We live in a society where we hear of kidnappings, car-jackings, suicide bombings. Depending on where we live, we don't dare leave our kids outside by themselves for even a minute.

Where does fear come from? We can fool ourselves into thinking that we're fearful because we live in a violent society on a war-torn planet. It's a scary place, this world. But fear is not just a post 9-11 phenomenon. It has always been a temptation to human beings. In the late 1990s, many people were fearful and worried about "Y2K." They bought generators and stored water, food, and other supplies because of dire warnings that all the computers in the world would shut down at midnight, January 1, 2000, bringing life as we know it to a grinding halt.

I remember refusing to buy into the Y2K thing but still feeling a vague uneasiness even as we made travel plans. We spent the turn of the century in Disney World with my parents and my kids. If the world was going to end, at least we'd all be together. Of course, as it turned out, we had a great time.

What are you afraid of? Maybe, like Laura and many others, you're afraid of other people's disapproval.

I am tempted to be fearful even when there don't seem to be any storm clouds on the horizon of my life. Sometimes my fears are so far below the surface I don't even know what they are. Most people think of me as confident and assertive, even willing to take risks. However, that comes not from my own strength but because I am called by God. I love the command God gives Joshua after Moses dies and he's to take over as leader of the children of Israel. "Have I not commanded you? Be strong and courageous. Do not be terrified; do not be discouraged, for the LORD your God will be with you wherever you go" (Josh. 1:9).

Strength and courage are not things we simply ought to wish for; they are character traits God has commanded us to embrace. Not always easy, is it? But if we look at the context of the verse above in Joshua, God doesn't just tell Joshua "chin up." He tells him how to be courageous.

First, God promises that he will "never leave you or forsake you" (Josh. 1:5). However, it's easy for us to forget that promise, or think it is not true, especially when life gets hard or the world seems to be just too violent and scary. God knows that, because the human race has always had a tendency toward violence and a tendency to fear that violence. That's why God gave Joshua and his people a strategy for courage, not just a command. What's the strategy? "Do not let this Book of the Law depart from your mouth; meditate on it day and night, so that you may be careful to do everything written in it. Then you will be prosperous and successful" (Josh. 1:8).

We tend to think of success mainly in financial terms. That's far too narrow a definition. For Joshua, it meant carrying out the mission God had given him: to lead the Israelites and to take over the land God had promised him. It meant he would have to wage war; he would have to fight, but God would be with him.

He couldn't do it on his own strength or by the power of positive thinking. He had to fill his mind and thoughts with God's truth. Fear is based on lies. Courage comes when you know the truth.

You will know the truth, and the truth will set you free. Free to courageously follow God's call. Whether you realize it or not, you are called by God. You may not be fighting physical battles, but you are fighting a battle for your heart and for your children's hearts. Be strong and courageous.

God has removed our heart of stone and given us a clean heart, a good heart. Our decisions, our priorities with regard to the use of our time, talents, and treasures should be based on that calling, not on fear.

Jesus kept saying, "Don't be afraid," because he knew that in this world, we'll have trouble and it will make us fearful. Some people feel occasional vague uneasiness or get scared in stressful situations. But for many others, panic attacks and extreme anxiety are a regular part of life. Millions of Americans take antidepressants to help them cope with their fear and anxiety.

While I don't suffer from depression, sometimes fear crops up at the most unexpected times. Whenever I have to travel or when someone I love has to travel, I feel a bit of fear: what if I never see them again? When my husband is late getting home, anxious thoughts flit across my brain: What if he's been in an accident? These fears generally move in and out so fast I hardly have time to tell myself, "Don't worry."

We live in a scary world, but one that is very uncomfortable with letting people be the least bit anxious or upset. I remember sitting in a dentist chair, which is enough to make most people feel a bit nervous. We don't have dental insurance, and I had just found out I needed two crowns on my teeth. I started imagining having to tell my husband about the cost. The cost was the scary part, not the actual work the dentist was about to perform.

The dentist went on explaining what he intended to do to my teeth, and I started to cry. I couldn't stop. Being reclined in the dentist's chair, the tears were running into my ears. "Are you okay?" he asked. His assistant sat me up and gave me a tissue, and I vainly struggled to stop the tears. I just was so worried about the cost of this work, even though it was a bit irrational to be that worried. It would be a big hit in the budget, but we could manage it. But still, I couldn't stop crying.

"I'm sorry," I blubbered.

"It's all right. Do you have panic attacks often?" the assistant asked me.

"What?!" I said. "I'm not having a panic attack!"

"You should talk to your doctor," she continued. "They have medication that can help you."

I wanted to rip off my little blue bib and run away. Could it be that part of the reason so many people are on medication for anxiety is that they don't want to feel their fear, and they listen to well-intentioned people like that assistant who tell them that one moment of fear means they need medication?

I recently found this in the newspaper: "Feeling stressed? More and more people are, and they're easing their tension by popping antidepressants known as 'selective serotonin reuptake inhibitors' (SSRIs) found in such drugs as Paxil, Prozac, Zoloft and Celexa. In 2003, some 142 million prescriptions were written for SSRIs in the United States. Yet 20 percent to 30 percent of patients aren't helped by such drugs, says Dr. Alexander Bodkin, assistant professor of psychiatry at Harvard Medical School."[1] The article suggested that learning and employing good coping skills, including moderate regular exercise, can be very effective in warding off depression.

I'm not saying antidepressants are bad. They are sometimes helpful and necessary to correct chemical imbalances, which many people suffer from. But they also have many side effects. I think we need to use discernment, especially in a society as overmedicated as ours.

It is easy to give in to fear. It has become normal to look for a pill or quick fix to take away our anxiety. But pills don't always help. The single most oft-repeated command in the Bible is "Fear not." God did not give us a spirit of fear, the Bible says (see 2 Tim. 1:7). So if God didn't give it to us, how did we get it?

From looking at the power of the Evil One, that's where. It's hard not to notice evil and pain because it is everywhere. If we focus on the wars and strife and evil of this world, we will live in fear. The prevalence of anxiety so deep that it requires medication shows how strong the grip of evil is in our world. It's easy to forget that we are children of God, deeply loved. Or to feel guilt if we have trouble believing it, which leads us to more fear and despair. We believe the lies the Evil One whispers in our ear: if only you had more faith, you'd be healthy and strong.

Don't believe the lies. You are a child of God. You are called by name, and you've been given a spirit of power, love, and a sound mind. Focusing on who you are in Christ is one of the best "coping skills" you can develop.

You belong to the one who has overcome, and you don't have to be afraid. That's why the single focus on Christ is not just a good idea; it is powerful. The practice of simplicity doesn't just clean our closets, it banishes fear from our hearts, because it puts our focus on the transforming power of perfect love, and perfect love casts out fear (see 1 John 4:18).

Don't forget that. Keep your focus on Jesus. You are a child of your loving heavenly Father, who has your best interest at heart. He really does.

Breathing Exercise

What anxieties, worries, responsibilities cause you to forget that you are a child of God, deeply loved? What are you afraid of? Even if your fear is irrational, name it. Pray for the strength and courage that only God can give you.

Look up some of the verses mentioned in this chapter (Isa. 43:1; Josh. 1:5–9; 2 Tim. 1:7; Ezek. 36:26; Ps. 51:10; James 4:7–8; and 1 John 4:18). Copy them in a journal or on note cards and read them every day for the next couple weeks. Take a deep breath as you read each Scripture verse. Notice what happens to your heart. Do you feel more fear, or less?

4

simplified

How can I focus on what matters?

"I've always been involved in a lot of things," admits Jean. "I have a high capacity to do things and a strong desire to have what I do be significant. I'm also a feeler in that I care a lot about what other people are experiencing. That combination can be crazy-making if you don't have any boundaries."

Jean's journey toward simplicity has been one of developing those boundaries and using them to filter out the loud voices of well-intentioned advice so she could listen to God's still, small voice.

Jean was married for nine years before she had her first child. "That's when the voices start, telling you what you ought to do: you ought to quit work, or no, you shouldn't quit work, or you should do what you want, or any number of things."

She chose to keep working. At the time, she was the administrator for the programming department (which encompassed the arts and worship) at a very large church. "It was very demanding and full time," she said. It was, in scope, responsibility, and pressure, much more like a corporate operations director job than a typical "church job."

Job Challenges

When Jean was expecting her first child, the church offered her a job as the programming director for its two midweek worship services. She would be responsible for designing the service, overseeing rehearsals, and coordinating all the different elements of the worship service (which songs to sing, visual elements, and drama) to support whatever the pastor was preaching on that night. It would be a high-visibility job that would use her creativity and leadership skills and stretch them.

"I asked if I could do it part-time," she says. "That was hard to even ask. But I was starting to realize what was healthy for me. I didn't have to reach the ceiling every day. It was too exhausting."

Part of Jean's exhaustion was due to her desire for excellence in all she did. She cared so much about the quality of her work and her parenting that she sacrificed basic things such as sleep.

"I had no Sabbath, not enough self-care," she says. "Combine that with someone who wants to be there for people who needed me, and then on top of that, throw a kid in the mix, and you get tired."

When Jean had her second child, she said the voices got louder. "Some people said you can't work with two kids at home; others said I should. I wanted my life to make a difference. I came to this place where I decided that the most significant question I could ask was just, 'What would please God most?' And what I heard from God was simply, 'What do you want to do?'"

She wanted to continue to work, feeling strongly that God was calling her to continue in the ministry she was working in. "It becomes easier to seek after God if you run everything through the grid of 'What is he calling me to do?'" she says.

For Jean, that is the heart of simplicity—to seek after God's kingdom, to do what he's called us to do, "rather than trying to attain some picture or standard we put in our heads," as Jean puts it. "One of the freeing things about simplicity is that you can stop the voices."

With freedom comes responsibility, because life doesn't stop changing, according to Jean. You have to keep adjusting and figuring out how to follow God. "So many people avoid simplicity as a discipline because they think they will have to give everything up. Well, you do, in a way, but you gain so much more."

When she first heard a pastor at her church talk about simplicity, "I thought, yeah, I dare you to make that work in my life," she says.

But as she looked at some of her friends who had begun to simplify and slow down their lives, "I wanted the peace and confidence that they seemed to have," she says.

For her, the journey of simplicity meant continuing to do her job and being firm about not working more than the twenty-two hours per week that she and the church had agreed to.

"Sometimes, that meant letting go of things that it would have made sense to hold on to, things that would have allowed me to impress people," she says. "It's hard. If you say no to an assignment, they might not ask again. You might not be considered a team player."

More Challenges

When Jean's second child, Sam, was about two years old, she began to notice that he was very different from her first child and different from most of his peers.

"He wasn't the kind of kid who wanted to play with other kids," she says. "He'd talk to adults but not socialize with other kids. And he'd do this thing, we didn't know what it was, so we called it his 'happy dance.' He'd jump and flap his arms. It's a classic sign of autism, but we didn't know it at the time."

Sam also was very picky about food and how his clothes felt, which Jean now realizes has to do with "sensory integration" issues. He was a bit uncoordinated, which she later realized is because he has low muscle tone, again another sign of his developmental challenges.

But he was very verbal and bright. "Academically, Sam didn't really need preschool. Yet socially, he was not at the same level as the other kids. The teacher wanted to hold him back because he couldn't cut very well," Jean says. "He had a hard time with the scissors. He couldn't cut, but he was reading."

Jean and her husband, Robert, decided that another year of preschool probably would not help Sam, since the teacher was not likely to spend all of her time teaching him to use scissors or helping him get along with others on the playground.

Jean's job continued to be demanding, as did continued challenges with Sam. He was bright, but he acted out. He seemed so precocious in some ways but struggled with basic tasks. Most frustrating was that Jean did not know what was causing the problems.

"We were seeing doctors and trying to figure out what was wrong," Jean says. "We were seeing a counselor about our parenting, because we thought we were doing something wrong. We learned a lot about parenting, but the counselor didn't get to the root of the problem. Even before Sam was in kindergarten, we had been seeing doctors, but it didn't help. Once he was even 'flapping' in the pediatrician's office, and the doctor just said he seemed kind of anxious."

A friend recommended another doctor, who wisely suggested that they stop trying to treat individual symptoms and "treat the whole person." He referred them to a specialist in developmental disorders for comprehensive testing.

Sam was diagnosed at age six with Pervasive Developmental Disorder (PDD). Doctors told Jean that PDD was similar to autism and other disorders but that Sam would make progress if he had physical and occupational and speech therapy. He needed to go to each of these separate therapy sessions every week.

As if this challenge were not enough, Jean's husband lost his job at about the same time. He found a new job quickly, but instead of being less than ten minutes from home, his new job involved more than an hour commute each way.

"Life always gets more complex," Jean says. She knew with her husband's new job that more of the care and getting Sam to therapy would fall on her. But financially, they still needed to have both of them working. Robert set up his schedule to start work at 6:00 a.m. so he could be home by 4:30 or 5:00 p.m. to spend time with the boys.

Caring for two small children, one of whom had special needs, along with working in a demanding job, made life a bit crazy. Jean even considered quitting her job, despite the financial pressure this might cause. She and Robert invited two other couples who knew them well to talk over their situation. "We told them we weren't going to make a decision that night, but we were interested in what they thought," she recalls.

After the friends had gone home that evening, Jean looked at her husband and said, "Well, it looks like I'm quitting." He shook his head. "He told me that our friends didn't see how much my job brings us as a family. He said, 'They don't know how much it blesses you and how much it makes you a better wife and parent.' So I came back to the question that I continually ask myself: how are we going to do life? Because that's the heart of simplicity: it's listening not just to God's call to do a specific thing but his call to a way to live."

Jean says that the "way to live" means she makes decisions based on obeying God, rather than listening to the voices of others who try to tell her what she ought to do. She has kept her focus on God by spending time alone with him. This requires discipline. Although she is more of a night person, she forces herself to get to bed before 11:00 p.m. so she can get at least seven hours of sleep and still be able to get up before the boys.

"If I can get up before the kids and spend time with God, that helps," she says. "It's good for me to start my day by saying that I'm available, that I want to be moving in the direction God wants me to go."

Paying Attention to Your Soul

As the boys got older and started school, Jean agreed to increase her hours at work to about thirty-five per week but refused to go full time.

"I knew my boundaries and where I had to draw the line, even psychologically," she says. "As I grew older, I became more aware of how much I needed solitude and rest. I needed more time with significant people in my life, rather than just more activities."

Then things began to change at work; the department was reorganizing. Jean wasn't sure what that meant, but eventually it became clear that she would need to step up to full-time work, which would likely take more than forty hours a week, if she was going to keep her job.

"I knew I needed to do something that would work in the life of my kids," she says. "I felt like what I was doing was useful, but life was very full."

She took three days off to think things over. "I was emotionally drained, so I took some time to rest and try to be quiet."

Jean loved her job and felt God used her to touch people's lives through it. But she wanted to give her children and family what they needed. During her three days away, "I journaled, I read, I walked, I cried. I asked God, 'What do you want from me?'" She talked to several people who knew her well, including a spiritual mentor who told her, "This is a major time of change. Don't do anything drastic. Make a change, but make one in which you can pay attention to your soul."

Financially, the family needed Jean's income, or at least part of it. After taking a good look at their finances, Jean and Robert decided they could cut back and live frugally wherever they could if Jean could find a more flexible part-time job.

The church offered her the chance to transition her part-time job into a consulting role. She would do the work of a worship director but as an independent contractor. She decided to take it. She has found other opportunities to do marketing and creative consulting as well. Moving to self-employment has allowed her to keep working and earning but provides much more flexibility because she can do it from home.

"I'm doing some work with nonprofits but also with a law firm. I'm producing some videos for another company," she says. "Financially, it's a risk because it's not a move up. But it offers me more freedom to be available for the kids. When they go back to school in the fall, I work more."

While they've had to make some cutbacks in spending, the flexibility is worth it, Jean says. Living frugally allows her to be available more often to the boys.

"It's not like we ever had an extravagant budget. But we've never had debt, so that helped. God has provided."

For instance, one day Robert came home and told her that the car needed four hundred dollars' worth of repairs. Jean noted that the work project she'd done for the few days before that had earned almost precisely that.

"At first, I thought, *There goes that money I just made.* But my perspective is changing. Instead of saying, 'I can't believe I had to spend that money as soon as I earned it,' I'm learning to say thank you to God for providing the work and the income so that I could use it as we needed it," she says.

Jean seems to have discovered that listening to God and trusting him will give us that illusive thing so many of us think we'll find at the mall: contentment.

These days, Jean says she's trying to "figure out a rhythm of rest and activity that works for us." In other words, she is trying to listen to God's direction on what Sabbath Simplicity should look like in her family. Most weekends, that means not scheduling more than one thing. For example, if they go to a party on Saturday night, they will say no to invitations to do something Friday night or Sunday.

"I'm getting better at saying no to things, and I don't feel compelled to always give a reason why. We're figuring out the boundaries," Jean says. "The result is that I'm a more joyful person."

Breathing Exercise

Sit and take a few slow, deep breaths. As you read Jean's story, what thoughts came to mind? What life challenges have you faced that have made your life more complicated? Could these same challenges be God's way of calling you to the simplicity that comes from focusing on him? Ponder that paradox for a while.

Complicated Simplicity

"Simplicity" is the cry of our culture. There are books, magazines, websites, and television programs focusing on simplicity. We desperately want to simplify our lives, but we are not sure how. We read Jean's story, or Laura's, and think, *Okay, I want a simpler life, but I'm not sure I want the pain or the hard work that might come with it.* Simplicity is in some ways rather complicated.

This creates, of course, a bit of anxiety. It also creates an opportunity for those who want to market books and websites and magazines on simplicity. The magazine *Real Simple*, for example, purports to tell people how to live a simple life, although its helpful tips on housekeeping and de-cluttering are interspersed with glossy ads for such essentials as pink leather purses, one-hundred-dollar baby sweaters, and high-heeled pumps.

We live at a time when technology and information are changing at an ever-increasing pace. Because I have so much information at my fingertips, it's easy to become overwhelmed. My fingertips are not that big.

Because of this and many other factors, everyone seems to be longing for simplicity. These days, ironically, we can find it at the mall. I bought a set of Pure Simplicity face cleanser and moisturizers the other day. There is a fragrance called Simply Happy, and isn't that what we all want, really?

If you search for just "Simplicity" on Amazon, you'll find 46,000 titles. Google it and you'll find 300,000 sites, from sewing patterns to business theory to extreme frugality. It's somewhat ironic how many different definitions and perspectives there are on simplicity. Simplicity is not so simple after all.

But it is possible. The Sabbath Simplicity lifestyle is one you can live, if you are willing to listen to God and focus on, as Jean puts it, the "way to live" that he's calling you to. There are not ten easy steps, but you can learn from others the right questions to ask.

Many modern Christians are not aware of simplicity as a Christian discipline. They think simplicity is a perfume, a magazine, or a method for organizing closets. They have been influenced, in varying degrees, by a "gospel of wealth" philosophy. They've heard television preachers tell them to "name it and claim it"; they've thought that if they use the "Power of Positive Thinking" they'll get what they want. They've read books on prayer and figured they could learn how to manipulate God into filling their orders, as if he were working at the drive-through window at McDonald's. ("Can you supersize those blessings and hold the pain and suffering, please?")

It's easy to assume that the truest barometer of God's favor on our lives is material blessings and pain-free living, where things always seem to go our way. I know I fall into this type of thinking. I know deep down that that thinking is based not on truth but on wishful thinking. God is not running some kind of celestial e-Bay, where we can simply search for whatever we want and put in a bid.

Here's a promise Jesus made that you can "name and claim": "In this world you will have trouble." Thanks a lot, right? But Jesus continues: "But take heart! I have overcome the world" (John 16:33).

Overcoming is not about avoiding pain but facing trials head-on, with our focus not on the problems but on Jesus. For Jean, dealing with a special-needs child is not something she thought she could handle, but keeping herself focused on Jesus and trying to be like him is what helps her handle it.

Looking for a true understanding of simplicity? Our focus is what makes our life simple. Both Laura and Jean would say that's what kept things simple when life was difficult.

I often feel I ought to simplify or that I've just got to get organized! It's easy to equate simplicity with de-cluttering or even a sparse, minimalist decorating style. If we limit our practice of simplicity to our housekeeping efforts, we miss out on a way of being with God that can make him more real and more relevant than we've ever experienced before.

Breathing Exercise

What do you think of when you hear the term "simplicity"? Have you ever thought of how it might relate to your spiritual life? What would a life of simplicity look like if your focus was consistently on Jesus and not on your circumstances? How might it be related to your spiritual life?

The Single Eye

Here's what Jesus taught about simplicity: "Do not store up for yourselves treasures on earth, where moth and rust destroy, and where thieves break in and steal. But store up for yourselves treasures in heaven, where moth and rust do not destroy, and where thieves do not break in and steal. For where your treasure is, there your heart will be also" (Matt. 6:19–21).

Jesus is not trying to be a killjoy. (He rarely is.) Instead, he's trying to tell us how to find real joy. And, despite the claims of *Real Simple* magazine, joy is not found at the mall . . . not even the outlet mall!

How much time do you spend shopping for things you really don't need? How much time do you spend maintaining your stuff? How many trips do you have to make to the Container Store to buy bins and baskets to put all your stuff in? How often do you have to sort through all the junk and have a garage sale or leave a few boxes on the porch for the Veterans' Association to pick up? "Storing up" implies hoarding, accumulating for the sake of simply having a lot. Unfortunately, storing up treasures on earth is our national pastime, and truly heeding Jesus's advice is not very easy. How much stuff is too much?

I understand the comfort of what some call "retail therapy." As Laura observed, it's a very socially acceptable way to self-medicate. I have even indulged in it myself. I understand wanting to have things. But what do we need and what do we simply want? How can we decide how much is enough?

There are, of course, no easy answers to these questions. Before we address the "how much" question, we need to look at the second part of what Jesus says. He sets up a contrast—don't do this; rather, do that. Don't hoard earthly treasure; store up treasure in heaven. How do we do that?

I've heard some people say that Jesus means we ought to do good deeds in this life so we'll earn brownie points (treasures) in heaven. If you're strongly evangelical, maybe you think it has to do with leading people to Christ, which means Billy Graham will have the biggest mansion in heaven. Maybe . . . but I don't think that's a complete picture. (No offense, Billy.) While we should try to act as Jesus would in a way that's loving and kind, God's favor cannot be earned. While we should tell others about him, our motivation should not be earning brownie points but sharing the joy that is within us. So what does it mean to store up treasures in heaven?

I think of it in terms of investment. What can I invest my time and energy in that will last? And the Bible is pretty clear that the only thing that will last into eternity is relationships. What do you really treasure, when it comes down to it?

My kids, my husband, my friends, these are treasures that matter to me. Jesus, my friend and leader, is the best treasure of all. He's the pearl of great price, and his love permeates not only my relationship with him but also my relationships with the people he's given me. People are more important than stuff. When it comes down to it, which is more valuable: my daughter or my diamond?

Jesus makes a curious statement in the next verse, Matthew 6:22. He says, "The eye is the lamp of the body. If your eyes are good, your whole body will be full of light."

What do good eyes have to do with where your treasure is or with where your heart is?

A lot.

The King James Version translates Jesus's statement this way: "The light of the body is the eye: if therefore thine eye be single, thy whole body shall be full of light."

What is a "single eye"? Even the old-fashioned King James English doesn't quite capture it as well as the original language of the Bible. Richard Foster wrote about it this way: "It refers both to a single aim in life and to a generous unselfish spirit. The two ideas have such a close connection in the Hebrew mind that they can be expressed in a single phrase. Singleness of purpose toward God and generosity of spirit are twins."[1]

What does it mean when we say someone has a "singular focus"? It means they are not easily distracted from their purpose or whatever their attention is focused upon. Where your focus is, that's where your heart is. That's where your treasure is.

Jesus says our focus should be him. That will result in both a singular focus and the generous spirit implied in Jesus's words.

In John 15, he told his followers, "Abide in me," or "Remain in me." The idea is to stay connected and focused on Christ. To walk with him, to love him, to listen to him. John 15:10 says, "If you obey my commands, you will remain in my love."

So abiding, according to Jesus, is about obedience. What rules are we to follow? John 15:12 makes it clear: "My command is this: Love each other as I have loved you."

If we are focused on Christ, if he is the treasure of our hearts, we will arrange our lives around that singular focus. We will desire to see him more clearly. And he tells us how to sharpen that focus: love others. Love others. Have a generous and unselfish spirit. When relationships with God and others are our treasures, we are free to live our values; people are more important than stuff.

What about my stuff? Does that mean I should get rid of all my material possessions? No. But when we begin to shift our focus, stuff becomes less appealing.

Breathing Exercise

Take a moment to breathe. Quiet your heart; sit in silence. Breathe and ask God to be present to you. Read the verses from John 15 very slowly. "If you obey my commands, you will remain in my love. My command is this: Love each other as I have loved you."

Linger over Jesus's words for several minutes. What does he want you to know? What might he be inviting you to do?

Contentment

"I know what it is to be in need, and I know what it is to have plenty. I have learned the secret of being content in any and every situation, whether well fed or hungry, whether living in plenty or in want," writes the apostle Paul in Philippians 4:12. And what is Paul's secret? "I can do everything through him who gives me strength" (Phil. 4:13). A relationship with Jesus is his source of contentment.

When we say we long for a simpler life, what does that mean? What I am looking for (and I think a lot of other people are too) is contentment. To be simple is to be free from grasping for more and consuming endlessly. It's about being content. The easy yoke, the way of life that Jesus invites us into, is not about striving and straining; it is about walking together with him, knowing that what we have and what we do is enough, and feeling content with that. Paul gives us a clue about the connection between simplicity and contentment that is found in Jesus.

The Bible says Jesus often talked with people about money and how it impacted them spiritually. Mark 10:17–22 tells the story of a wealthy young man who asks how he can inherit eternal life. At first, Jesus meets him where he's at and tells him to obey God's law. This self-deceived man says he's always kept every one of those rules. Jesus, who knew that he hadn't, doesn't contradict him. In fact, the text says, "Jesus looked at him and loved him" (v. 21). But it's a tough love, one that challenges this eager young man.

Jesus then says: sell all your possessions, give the money to the poor, and then come back and we'll talk. We can learn a lot about this man's priorities by both the way he phrases the question and the way he reacts to Jesus's answer. First, his question: "What must I do to inherit eternal life?" (v. 17). In other words, he's thinking, *I've inherited a lot, I've accumulated a lot. This is something that's missing from my portfolio. I need to get this. Just tell me how.* He'd been following the rules (or so he thought), but he wasn't sure if that was enough.

He was in acquisition mode. It may be that Jesus's answer was inspired in part because of the way the young man asked it. Jesus doesn't make this a blanket statement for all who want to follow him. But he did want to shift this man's thinking.

In the end, however, the man goes away sad, because Jesus was in essence telling him that the one thing he didn't have, he couldn't acquire in the way he'd acquired other things. Instead of getting, he would need to give.

He was also sad because he realized Jesus had seen right through his lie about keeping every commandment. I think the unspoken comment in Jesus's answer is: "You've kept every commandment? Really? How about the first one: 'You shall have no other gods before me'? It seems like money is your god. So get rid of that god."

Come and learn from me, Jesus says to the rich young man. This upwardly mobile guy wasn't just sad at the idea of having to give away all that money. His facade had been seen through; Jesus had unmasked him.

I don't feel very wealthy, but compared to most of our planet, where over a billion people live in abject poverty, I am incredibly well off. If Jesus asked me to sell all I had and give the money to the poor, I would feel sad too . . . and probably pretty scared. I like my stuff, and I like the way I get to live. I live in a safe neighborhood with good schools, in the wealthiest country in the world.

If we have a roof over our head and food to eat, we are way ahead of most people on the planet. If we are this wealthy (although it may not feel like "wealth" to us), it may be indeed that God has "blessed" us. However, we often forget that God blesses us not so we can get fat but so we can share our abundance with others.

Voluntary Simplicity

Interestingly, thinkers outside (or on the fringes) of the mainstream Christian tradition have preached simplicity with more fervor than the church in recent decades. Often people who are acting out of a concern for the environment are more deliberate about simplicity than most Christians.

In 1981, Duane Elgin's book *Voluntary Simplicity* urged people (especially Americans) to live a deliberately unmaterialistic lifestyle that used fewer of the world's resources: "We can describe voluntary simplicity as a manner of living that is outwardly more simple and inwardly more rich, a way of being in which our most authentic and live self is brought into direct and conscious contact with living. This way of life is not a static condition to be achieved, but an ever-changing balance that must be continuously and consciously made real. Simplicity in this sense is not simple. To maintain a skillful balance between the inner and outer aspects of our lives is an enormously challenging and continuously changing process. The objective is not to dogmatically live with less, but is a more demanding intention of living with balance in order to find a life of greater purpose, fulfillment and satisfaction."[2]

Jean has never read Elgin's book, but I think he pretty accurately describes how she has chosen to live her life. She has given a lot of thought to balancing the inner and outer aspects of her life. Elgin says the secret to an inwardly rich life is to know when to say, "Enough."

Elgin's philosophy to pursue that which is outwardly simple but inwardly rich echoes Jesus's exhortation to get your heart and your treasure in line. Elgin's thinking spawned a movement that is not just concerned with the environment but also with the gap between rich and poor.

"If the world is profoundly divided materially, there is very little hope that it can be united socially, psychologically, and spiritually. Therefore if we intend to live together peacefully as members of a single, human family, then each individual has a right to a reasonable share of the world's resources,"[3] Elgin writes. We might tend to dismiss people like this as idealistic tree-huggers, but we can and should learn something from them. And we ought to notice that his ideas are remarkably similar to those lived out by the early church, which of course, was trying to put into practice the teachings of Jesus.

Joe Dominguez and Vicki Robin, in their best-selling book *Your Money or Your Life: Transforming Your Relationship with Money and Achieving Financial Independence,* urged readers to rethink their financial priorities. They dared to speak back to the upwardly mobile yuppie culture of that time, challenging the assumption that chasing the almighty dollar was the path to happiness.

They preached a message of frugality based on their observation that once our standard of living reaches a certain point, our satisfaction with more stuff falls off; yet we often keep striving for more, if only out of habit or because everyone else is doing so. They urged readers to find the place that was actually "enough" and recognize it, so that they could enjoy life instead of continuing to chase after something they already had achieved. Have you ever thought about how much is "enough"? Most people, no matter how much they make, will say that "enough" is just a little more than they currently have. As a result, contentment eludes them.

In contrast, Dominguez and Robin urged people to be frugal, not only for the sake of the poor, but because it was actually more enjoyable: "Frugality means we are to enjoy what we have. If you have ten dresses but still feel you have nothing to wear, you are probably a spendthrift. But if you have ten dresses and have enjoyed wearing all of them for years, you are frugal. Waste lies not in the number of possessions but in the failure to enjoy them. Your success at being frugal is measured not by your penny-pinching but by your degree of enjoyment of the material world."[4]

Here's what Dominguez and Robin observed about America in the early 1990s: "Greed is . . . a socially acceptable and even encouraged motivation. . . . Our society, with its skewed distribution of wealth, rewards greed over need— so much so that it seems slightly un-American to suggest that the poor deserve at least a small piece of the action."[5]

A fringe of society listened to these and other writers in the late twentieth century, and the "Voluntary Simplicity" movement was born. When the movement started, it was extremely countercultural.

This is no longer just a fringe movement. Amazon.com lists nearly one hundred books on the topic of Voluntary Simplicity. There are numerous websites on the Voluntary Simplicity movement and Simplicity Circles (which are support and discussion groups). There's even a website preaching frugality and selling products to help you live frugally (okay, that's just a little bit ironic), called the Simple Living Network.

While I've found that the principles espoused by the Voluntary Simplicity movement are thought-provoking, even helpful, the ideas seem incomplete. Yes, this type of simplicity can help you slow down and create more space in your life, but space for what? A vague spirituality or sense of responsibility for the planet? That is not enough for me. That's why it helps me to talk with someone like Jean, who reminds me that simplicity is about running every decision through the "God's will" grid, not just frugality or organizing or eating organic vegetables.

Breathing Exercise

How connected are the financial and spiritual areas of your life? What keeps them separated? Are you afraid that Jesus might give you the same direction he gave the rich young man? What small steps can you take to cut back on your consumption and spending so that you are able to share with others in need? If you feel resistant to this idea, don't fret; that is normal. But don't dismiss it either. Take a deep breath, and then spend some time journaling and thinking about the fear and resistance that you feel. Remember that Jesus looked at the rich young man and loved him, and he loves you too.

Cutting Back

If you have the means to eat more than one bowl of rice and beans per day, you are better off than much of the world's population, including people in the United States.

According to the U.S. Census Bureau, 7.2 million families (or 9.6 percent of the population) in the United States lived in poverty in 2002 (the poverty threshold is defined as $18,392 in annual income for a family of four). The number of people in severe poverty increased from 13.4 million in 2001 to 14.1 million in 2002.

I'm not saying you have to solve the problems of the world. You can't. The statistics, being put in millions and billions of people, can be totally overwhelming. But they are important because they provide perspective. If you could afford to buy this book, you are not living in abject poverty. You have a lot . . . and so do I.

But if you still feel as if you don't have enough, you may be living beyond your means. And the pressure you feel to pay the bills is very real. You might need to examine your lifestyle, even if you don't think it is all that extravagant. You might need to think about living on a budget. God may want you to prune more than your schedule.

The Bible doesn't say wealth is wrong. It simply says that people are a higher priority than possessions. God invites us into a life where we're not focused on accumulation or consumption but on the joy of loving him and loving his people. When God blesses us, we should share with others. Look at the example of the first church, which was born at Pentecost, when the Holy Spirit came to the believers in Jerusalem after Jesus had risen and returned to heaven. Look at how they practiced simplicity: "All the believers were together and had everything in common. Selling their possessions and goods, they gave to anyone as he had need" (Acts 2:44–45).

The idea of leveling the ground between the haves and have-nots, whether we like it or not, is biblical. But in my comfortable suburban life, I am uncomfortable with even trying to figure out how to live that out. Certainly, I'm not just supposed to indiscriminately give away all I have. I don't think God is calling me to sign over my 401k to the homeless man holding a cardboard sign by the freeway entrance. Is he?

Rationalizations come easily to me as well. I tell myself that my standard of living has to do with the hard work my husband and I have done, not only in our jobs but also in being disciplined to live within our means. We have been very careful to avoid debt. We save and invest carefully.

The Bible urges us to be faithful stewards of what God has given us. That means making good choices about how we spend our money. God does not want us to hoard but rather to be frugal (wise) so we will have extra to share with those in need.

Breathing Exercise

Do you think of yourself as wealthy? According to the United Nations Department of Economic and Social Affairs, some 1.2 billion people around the planet (almost a quarter of the developing world's population) survive on less than $1 per day. How much more than that do you have? Do you have a car or multiple cars? A house? Food to eat? How do these privileges affect your dependence on God? How do they affect your level of gratitude?

The Gift of Space

Okay, maybe we can come to grips with limiting our stuff. But the big question for parents is: what about my kids' stuff?

Our children live in the same culture we do. They learn very early about getting stuff. If you ask kids what birthdays and Christmas are all about, they will typically say presents.

As parents, there are some steps we can take to fight the culture.

First, limit television, especially commercial television. Why? Advertising. The goal of the advertising industry can be summed up this way: to create discontent. If an advertiser is going to talk you into buying a new car, he's got to convince you that the car you have is no good. An advertiser's main objective is to make you unhappy with the stuff you have and to fool you into thinking that you will be happy if you buy the things they advertise. Is this what you want to build into your children?

Second, if your kids are very small, limit the number of toys you buy. Believe me, they will still accumulate a lot of toys via birthday parties and other occasions. Do you often find yourself buying things for your kids out of guilt? Kids may say they want a lot of stuff, and we often kowtow to their requests, but what they really crave is our attention and affection. Be generous with your time, but be careful with how much stuff you throw at them.

When you choose not to buy a bunch of stuff for your kids, you give God the opportunity to provide. You can create space for God, where he can show his power and love to you and your kids. That's what I've experienced.

When my son was born, I dressed him in some of his sister's old blue, green, and yellow sleepers. His grandmothers bought him a few outfits, delighted as they were to have a boy to shop for. (He was the first male grandchild on both sides of the family.)

I was especially grateful for their gifts, since my husband had lost his job just before Aaron was born. At that time, we had to live frugally. It wasn't a choice; it was a necessity. (A sort of involuntary simplicity, if you will.)

Anyway, a close friend had a baby boy three months before I did, and that first year, her child grew quickly. My friend would hand down her son's clothes as he outgrew them, just in time for Aaron to grow into them. Our finances were extremely tight at that time, and we were trusting God to provide for us. Those hand-me-downs were a tangible reminder of God's love for us.

Had I gone to the Gap and just bought things on credit, I would have missed out in several ways: One, I would have missed the opportunity to see God provide for our family. Two, I would not have had the opportunity to build a stronger relationship with my friend, who became very dear to me. Three, I would not have been able to teach my children that God does provide and new clothes are a luxury, not a necessity. And finally, I would have ended that year in debt (after buying clothes on credit), and I believe debt is something that keeps us from focusing on God, because it takes away a measure of our freedom.

As I look at that list, I realize that God is giving me treasures right now; I don't even have to wait for heaven!

I now make it a habit to hand down my kids' clothes and toys to friends and neighbors because I know how receiving this kind of thing blessed me. What surprises me is how I feel peace, joy, and contentment when I am the giver. Delivering a bag of toys and clothes to a friend is another way of storing up treasures in heaven.

So back to the big question: how much, or how little, is enough?

I agree with Dominguez and Robin's statement: "Waste lies not in the number of possessions but in the failure to enjoy them." Do you see your stuff as a blessing from God that you can enjoy and share? Does your stuff enhance relationships or detract from them?

Christian simplicity is about where we focus. Rather than focusing on accumulating stuff, attaining accomplishments, or moving up the career ladder, our focus is supposed to be on Christ. Now, with that focus, we still might have some things, we might accomplish some very good things, we might become successful in our career. But those things are not our main focus. The goal of simplicity is not just to reduce complexity. It is not simply about de-cluttering. Rather, it is following Jesus's advice to "seek first the kingdom of God, and all these things will be added unto you."

In other words, make following God your first priority, and everything else will fall into place. It's possible that you could get as much joy from giving something away as you did from having it.

Breathing Exercise

In an earlier book, I wrote: "Long before simplifying became something trendy for burned-out yuppies to embrace, heroes of the Christian faith were practicing it by embracing this concept of the 'single eye.' They weren't motivated by the desire for uncluttered closets—many of them didn't even have closets or even more than one set of clothes. Instead, they were motivated by a single purpose: loving God."[6] Do you see your stuff as a blessing from God that you can enjoy and share? Does your stuff enhance relationships or detract from them? Try giving away some of your stuff in the next week. See what it does to your heart.

part three

the reason

For I am gentle
and humble in heart

5

mindful

How can I live intentionally?

I remember watching my friend Donna leave church one weekday after doing some volunteer work. She and her kids headed toward the door while I was talking to someone. Twenty minutes later, I walked out and found her and her two preschool children crouched on the sidewalk, looking at bugs, not even halfway to their car in the parking lot. Donna looked up and smiled at me. "We don't move very fast, do we?" she laughed. She was not in a hurry to get home. She had set up her day so that there were not ten other places she "had to" get to, so she was able to simply be present. It was a nice day, and she was enjoying the moment with her children, enjoying their curiosity about the world. What could have been annoying if she had been hurried became a moment to remember.

What would happen to your relationship with your kids if you stopped telling them to hurry all the time? What if you took some time to share their wonder at the world? Often we are hurrying out of habit, and we don't stop to ask why. What are we saying to our kids? Hurry and get in the car; I really want to get home so I can start doing laundry and getting the house cleaned up. I can't wait to clean the toilets, so get a move on! Do we really want to rush home for *that*?!?

I didn't think so. So why do we rush; why do we tell the kids to hurry up? I don't know about you, but I like being in charge. If I say hurry and my kid does, I am in control. Letting my children set the agenda, as Donna did, requires a sort of quiet humility. It requires a gentle spirit, a love that does not demand its own way.

Recently when I had coffee with Donna, we talked about how she practices simplicity. It's something she's been doing for years, way before she had her children. She says moments like the one in the parking lot at church are commonplace in her life because she is ruthlessly unhurried.

"One of the benefits of getting married and having my kids later in life [in her late 30s] is that I had time on my own, and that provided a place for me to listen to God, to pay attention to what I loved and who I was, and not be influenced by other forces," she says.

Now her children are four and five years old. She is at home with them, although she volunteers about six to eight hours a week at church. The kids love to go to child care at church, where they see their friends. But that is the only thing on their schedule. They are not in any other activities.

"We purposely have large blocks of time open in our schedule," Donna says. "They are not in any outside activities right now because they have fun playing and pretending, and we value that."

As I talked with Donna, I noticed her using some words that hurried people don't use so often. Words like *pay attention* and *purposely*. One of the keys to simplicity is mindfulness. Being intentional, paying attention. It's about being present in the moment but also keeping the big picture in mind. Living mindfully means choosing carefully what you say no to and yes to, and knowing why you are doing so. Mindfulness allows you to see what would be the most gentle and loving response to any situation, and then being attentive enough to do it.

It's not enough to say that you value time for kids to develop their imagination; you actually have to put time for that in your schedule.

When her daughter was born, Donna continued working as a graphic artist part-time from home but found it difficult. "I'd be on the phone trying to talk about a project and just tossing little blocks at her to keep her distracted," she remembers. So she chose to say no to working for pay. Obviously, this is a decision she made with her husband. He was supportive of having her focus her efforts on their very young children.

When her son was born a year and a half later, Donna even said no to volunteering. "Just getting out of the house was really hard," she admits. Her most important practice at that time? "When Hallie was an infant, I was relentless about taking naps," Donna said. "If I didn't, I was just a mess. I was exhausted. It's just physically exhausting when they are little."

Again, Donna was simply paying attention. Simplicity requires mindfulness, and if you are too tired, you can't be mindful. When you're tired, you don't need to try harder.

You need a nap. Be gentle enough to yourself that you will give yourself a nap if you need it.

These days, Donna volunteers at church one day a week, designing and building drama sets and creating illustrations. Her volunteer work is related to what she did in the workplace but different enough that she is learning new things and nurturing that artistic side of herself that can easily get lost in the mundane chores of mothering.

"I love it," she says of her volunteer work. "I believe it's part of the reason God made me. I have a sense of calling. And it's good for our family. The kids get to be with their friends for six hours in an environment where people love them. I'm learning some new building and design skills, having fun, and also serving the church. But if the kids are sick, I can just call and say we can't come. It's the least stressful way to use my gifts."

Donna is grateful to have her husband's complete support. "We're a team," she says. He has always strongly encouraged Donna to be at home with the kids yet also supports her desire to develop her talents as an artist, whether by working, volunteering, or simply spending time drawing for pleasure.

One of the ways Gary expresses that support is by giving Donna Saturday mornings as time for herself. Balancing time for herself with "mom" time helps keep things in perspective.

"From the time I get up until about noon, Gary has the kids," she said. "In nice weather, I might go for a run or a walk. Usually I spend at least part of my Saturday morning at Starbucks, just reading or working on a project, which I love. Sometimes I'll go to the Botanic Gardens or another place of beauty."

Gary makes the morning count, usually taking the kids out to breakfast and then on some excursion, perhaps the zoo or a park. But the kids have his undivided attention for several hours, and Donna gets a break.

Donna says having some time each week helps her to be more patient, helps her to remember and live out her values. "I want my son to have time to sit and watch a roly-poly bug cross the driveway," she says. Donna's considering homeschooling her kids next year, but for now, "we focus just on reading and playing. If the kids get bored, they get to figure out what to do. If I don't get involved, they do better. When they complain about being bored, I just suggest they go to their room, open a closet door, and look on the shelves and see which toy or game catches their eye. The whining usually stops within about ten minutes, and then they stay engaged longer in whatever they end up doing because they've chosen it for themselves."

Notice that Donna is willing to put up with whining for longer than most of us. Also notice how that pays off. She doesn't solve her kids' problem—she has realized that her kids' boredom is their problem, not hers. And they "get to" solve it. It's a learning opportunity for them. She's patient, and the kids realize that they can solve the problem and find something interesting to do. The benefit for her kids is huge: they learn that they have the creative capacity to find something fun, to solve their own problems, to be a little independent. They take the whole journey from "I'm bored" to "I'm capable and creative," and all their mom did was tell them to stare at their toy shelf for a few minutes.

Parenting in this way requires being humble enough to not have to control every aspect of your child's day. It requires being gentle but firm, saying, "I know you can solve your problem" but not stepping in and solving it for them.

Before having kids Donna worked as a graphic designer and eventually as the director of a design department. She has illustrated books. She always knew she was an artist. "I'm lucky because I figured out early in life what I loved to do, and I did it," she said. "I know myself. I tend toward being quiet. Being an artist, I knew that I like visually simple things. So our house is visually simple," Donna says. No knickknacks, no excess junk on shelves, no ruffled, floral upholstery or complicated window treatments. "In fact, we're trying to streamline our house and even our garden so that it is low maintenance. Our goal is to not have to spend time on our house so that we can help others. We want to be able to help our neighbor with her yard rather than spending all our time getting stuff, cleaning stuff, storing stuff, fixing stuff."

Again, Donna and Gary are not just drifting into simplicity. They are mindful about it. The two of them regularly sit down and talk about their goals and where they are headed as a family. "We have family goals and dreams," Donna said. "We review those and talk about them regularly."

She and her husband are currently planning a vacation, just the two of them, where they will be able to do two things: "First, we want to just have fun, without the kids. Second, we want to spend some time evaluating where we are as a family, figuring out more clearly our values and mission as a family. We want to talk and dream about what we need to be, what our kids need. We just finished reading *Boundaries with Kids*[1] in our family group. It lists character qualities that every child needs. We want to talk specifically about how to develop those qualities in each of our kids."

For example, Hallie knows that her "job" is to love her little brother. When Hallie is being less than loving, Donna asks her, "What's your job, Hallie?" and she replies, "To love Cody." Once, frustrated with her little brother, she asked, "Can I have a different job?" Cody's job is "to be responsible." Donna says the fact that everyone in the family knows their "job" helps define expectations and is much better than just telling them to "behave" or "be good." Because she lives at a slower pace, she's able to catch the kids being good and point out when they are successfully doing their jobs—being loving or responsible. "What's your job?" is a much gentler way to guide your child's behavior than the method some parents use, which is to yell "Cut it out!" at their kids.

"Simplicity is the only way I can live," Donna said. "My brain shuts off if there is too much going on. I'm glad I had those years on my own, where I learned about myself, learned about how to live with others through the roommates I had. But Gary has provided a place where the best of me comes out. He's my soul mate. He helps me become so much healthier."

Simplicity is not just about pace of life but about staying focused on Christ, to live as gently and humbly as he would. Donna has adjusted the way she connects with God now that she is a mom.

"I used to get up every morning and read my Bible and journal," she said. "That's kind of dropped off a lot. But we've decided that there are things that are nonnegotiable. For instance, it's built into our schedule to go to church. Worship is a huge thing for me. We don't decide that day if we feel like going or not. We just always go. And also, I make sure I spend time outside. Being in creation is a spiritual practice for me and also for our family."

Donna is a great mom, but she felt a little trepidation when she first became a parent. She had loved her job and had felt it was a huge part of her identity.

She remembers that when Hallie was born, her mom came to help out for a few days. "That first day, it got to be lunchtime and I looked at my mother and said, 'Mom, there's no cafeteria here!' I had always worked and gone out to lunch or gone to the cafeteria, so I had no idea what to do!"

You may have guessed this, but Donna is not a big cook. When she was single, if she ate dinner at home it would often consist of cereal or perhaps chips and salsa. She says one of the things she and Gary want to do is have more family meals. Since he gets home at different times each night (and sometimes is out of town on business) because of his job, Donna often just feeds the kids when they get hungry. As a result, they don't typically sit down together as a family for dinner.

"We're trying to have a family meal just once a week," she said. "You'd think it wouldn't be that hard because the kids are small. But it is. It's so fun when we have it though. The kids love it."

Steps to Simplicity

God calls each of us to simplicity, but it won't look the same in your life as it does in Donna's or mine or anyone else's. What is the same, however, is that we journey toward deeper connection with him, with that "single eye" on Jesus.

Donna and Gary live frugally in both big and small ways. For example, they don't have cable television, not just because of the cost but because they want to limit the amount of time they spend watching TV.

They also live in a much smaller house than a mortgage broker would tell them they can "afford." They thought about moving to a bigger house but have now decided they'd rather stay where they are because it's easier to maintain, clean, and pay for a smaller house. A humbler house keeps life simpler.

They don't live this way simply to save money. If your focus is on frugality for frugality's sake, *not* spending money can quickly become a "god" as easily as spending money can. Donna and Gary say staying out of debt and not accumulating a lot of stuff is a way of living out their values. That implies, obviously, that they have talked about and know what those values are.

"We value the family unit," Donna explains. "We do discuss what might be best for the individuals in our family, but we also look at what is best for the family as a whole. At times those needs conflict, and we have to wrestle with that. We also value service and giving to others, living within our means, and using our gifts in our church."

Donna and Gary have found that living out those values is easier when they're not encumbered by too much stuff or too much debt.

"We're trying to forge clear values in our family so that as our kids and our family change, the values won't," Donna said.

Breathing Exercise

Frugality is a key component of Donna and Gary's commitment to simplicity. For some of us, simplifying means looking first at financial issues. For the more thrifty or frugal among us, it's less about money and more about issues behind our financial and other choices—issues like control and trust.

Frugality alone won't put your focus on Christ. It could just as easily put your focus on frugality. But sometimes your stuff (and your desire to accumulate more stuff or better stuff) gets in the way of your being able to clearly see Christ.

Ask yourself: What stands in the way of my being focused on Christ? How mindful am I? How could I live more humbly and gently? Where am I in regard to this simplicity thing? Where do I want to be?

What's Your Next Step?

One of my favorite Internet sites is Mapquest.com. Within a matter of seconds, I can get directions to any place I want to go.

If there were a spiritual Mapquest.com, where would you want to go? Maybe you want to have time to build meaningful friendships. Maybe you want to slow down enough to really enjoy your children's childhood. Maybe you'd just like to live a little more gently. Maybe you want your family to have a day of rest that you can share together. Maybe you want to be able to actually hear God when you pray, or maybe you just want to be able to pray. Maybe you want to learn to breathe, both physically and spiritually.

One thing you should know about Mapquest: you need more than just a destination. What happens if you click on "driving directions" but then only put in where you want to go? If you type in "Topeka, Kansas" as your destination but don't fill in the blank that tells where you are starting, you won't get your desired directions to Topeka.

You can only know what your next step is if you know where you are. If you are in Keokuk, Iowa, your route to Topeka will be different than if you are starting in New York City.

So, where are you? What is your next step toward Sabbath Simplicity? Unless you spend some time thinking about where you are, you can't possibly know which direction to move.

How do you know where you are? Look back at the questions in the "Breathing Exercise" sections of this book. When you were directed to be still and simply breathe, what was that like for you? If it was hard for you to be quiet for more than thirty seconds, then that's where you are. As one of my spiritual mentors likes to remind me, "You can't be anywhere except where you are."

Perhaps you've become aware that you never really look your children in the eye and listen to what they are saying. Perhaps your next step is to begin to change that, to show your love for them by paying attention in a new way. To humbly let go of your own agenda for even a few minutes, to focus on others, especially your kids.

Maybe you deeply desire a more meaningful relationship with God. Your next step might have you meditating on Scripture in a way that helps you get to know him better.

Once you know where you are, think again about where you want to go. What is your desire? Not what you think will impress others or what you think you are supposed to do to be a "good" person, but what you really want. What desire has God put in your soul with regard to your relationships with others and your connection with him?

Also, what is God calling you to do? We've talked about mission. Have you done the work of praying and waiting and listening to know what God wants you to do? Are you clear on your mission? That will also help you figure out your next step.

Moving toward that goal will take time. You don't have to figure out exactly how to get there. But you do have to determine, with God's help, what direction you should start off in. How do I get to Topeka? One step at a time. Which direction should I go? It depends on your starting point.

Where do you sense God is calling you to go? Maybe you're not supposed to go to Topeka but to Des Moines. Or maybe you don't know any more than the next step.

Maybe you're fairly certain about the direction God has called you to take, but you're thinking you'd like to take the journey at a slower pace. Or maybe you'd like to try rearranging things in order to have a Sabbath, a day or even half day of rest. You can't just screech to a halt and abandon all your obligations, as appealing as that sometimes sounds.

What you can do is be aware that you are looking for opportunities to say no, to slow down, if only for a little while.

Breathing Exercise

Sit quietly for a few minutes, taking slow, deep breaths until you feel yourself settling down. Where are you, spiritually speaking? Where do you want to go? Where do you sense God is calling you? What is your next step? Spend some time reflecting and journaling on these questions. Take your time. Write down a single next step that you think may bring you closer to a Sabbath Simplicity lifestyle. Ask for God's help in taking that step within the next week.

One Step Slower

One way to slow down is to actually take advantage of opportunities when you see them. That sounds obvious, but we often don't do it. If something in our busy schedule gets canceled, we rush to fill the now "free" time with some other obligation.

Recently, I had an opportunity to use some unexpected free time to connect with my son. Being the second child, he doesn't get as much interaction with me as my daughter. Experts say this is normal. They also recommend parents be intentional about spending one-on-one time with the children who, through no fault of their own, are simply not the firstborn child. That sounds like a great idea, but I don't always do it. You know how it is . . . you get busy. But this day, I was mindful of my son and of my desire to connect with him.

My daughter had a 6:30 p.m. soccer practice scheduled on this particular Friday, and I had planned to work dinner and chores around driving her to and fro. I was mindful of Aaron but not sure how I was going to connect with him while he spent a large chunk of his evening in the backseat of the minivan.

Another mom from the team called and offered to drive. Both ways. Really. She was going to be out taking her other children places anyway. A gift fell into my lap: no driving in Friday night rush hour and also time with my second-born, my quiet introvert. I breathed a prayer of thanks and gratefully accepted this gift. I resisted the urge to use the time to run other errands or even to clean the house. *If the reason I want to slow my life is to have more meaningful interactions with my family,* I thought, *then a great step in that journey would be to actually spend time with Aaron.*

Melanie ate her dinner quickly, jumping up and grabbing her soccer bag when the car horn sounded from the driveway. Aaron and I lingered over the rest of dinner. We talked, and not once was he interrupted by his sister. I asked him questions about his friends, his feelings, what was going on at school. I listened to his answers, looking at his face. He told me he's decided he likes reading, "because it helps your brain."

After dinner, we did not turn on the TV. We sprawled on the couch, he at one end with his *Magic Treehouse* book, me at the other end with *Voluntary Simplicity*. We read in utter, beautiful silence, the dog at our feet, a down afghan on our knees. I sometimes reached over and rubbed his feet. The only noise for quite a while was the sound of pages turning.

When he finished reading his book, I asked him to tell me about it. I put down my book, looked him in the eyes, and really listened. We lay on the couch together, snuggly, and talked. About him. For this little window of time, it was all about him. I asked, "Which do you like better, Aaron, being by yourself or in a big crowd?" He paused; I waited. I was mindful about not interrupting. As I waited, I prayed that God would keep my heart gentle. After a minute, Aaron said, "I like being with one person, or maybe two friends, or being alone. But not a big group." I responded, "Me too. I especially like to be with you." Aaron just smiled.

Later we searched the Internet for information about the Sears Tower, where he has chosen to take just two friends (instead of a big group) for his eighth birthday. We planned his party, besides the sightseeing: pizza, opening presents, a sleepover, homemade milk shakes in the blender. ("I don't like cake," he told me. "I can't put candles in milk shakes," I reminded him. "We can have muffins for breakfast," he says, "and you can put a candle in that." I smiled.) The friends will sleep over and have muffins and bacon and eggs for breakfast. "Ari likes eggs, Paul likes bacon," he explained. Okay. I found myself smiling again, enjoying the fact that even on his birthday, he was thinking about what his friends would like.

As he showered to get ready for bed, I thanked God for car pools and for the opportunity to relate directly, face-to-face, with my precious second-born, my only son. Sometimes I think of him as a little mirror, but he's more like a still pond; I see reflections of myself and my temperament. He resembles me in physical features, yet he is so much deeper, so much more. He is himself, a unique and amazing child. He's worth getting to know.

Breathing Exercise

As you go through the next few days, look for opportunities to slow down a little. Then actually take advantage of the opportunity. Go slower for an hour or a day. Say no, if only for a while. Be mindful in what you do. Notice what effect this has on your soul. Do you feel calmer, or perhaps anxious about all the things you are leaving undone? Take some time to breathe, to pray. Ask God for chances to slow down. If you make a regular habit of doing this, what might happen to your relationships with God and with other people?

Family Meals

Another step toward Sabbath Simplicity, toward a saner pace of life, is to share meals. It used to be that families shared meals every day, often more than once a day. That rarely happens anymore, in part because we think we don't have time. And because we really don't have time. By saying yes to hurry and overscheduling, by saying yes to something fun like Little League, we have unwittingly said no to having meals together.

Baseball games, soccer practices, and all kinds of other activities are often held at 5:00 or 6:00 p.m., in time for the coach who works a job full-time to get to the practice or game. It only gets worse when the kids get older.

Family meals were very important to me growing up. Even when I was in school, our whole family ate breakfast together before my brother and I ran to catch the bus. When we came home from school, my mom was there, which I realize even then was somewhat unusual. We had a snack, played outside or read a book, studied or maybe watched a little television, until 6:30 p.m., when my father walked in the door and we sat down to eat as a family. Every night.

Maybe you grew up this way, or maybe not. Maybe both your parents worked and an older sibling helped put dinner on the table. Maybe you were that older sibling. Maybe you had dinner at your mom's during the week and dinner at your dad's house (or with him at McDonald's) on the weekends. Maybe your house was not very peaceful, and you don't even know what a family meal looks like.

Now that I have a family of my own, things are a little different than they were in my family growing up. It's harder. My husband often works evenings. My kids have some activities, which are often in the early evening hours.

But even if it's just the kids and I, we make time for family dinners several nights a week. This requires some planning, but it is possible. I don't give up just because it isn't perfect; my husband is often not there because of work. Dinner is sometimes fried chicken or a pizza. Sometimes, as the kids have gotten older, one of them is not there either. But still I persevere, refusing to give up on this just because our meal can't look like a Norman Rockwell Thanksgiving. A meal is a connecting point, a place to pause. It might seem difficult at first to arrange, but it actually makes life simpler because it redirects my focus. Remember, simplicity is not about doing whatever takes the least effort. It's about staying focused on your priorities.

In this particular season of our lives, my daughter has soccer practice from 6:00 to 8:00 p.m. on Tuesday and Thursday. Driving to her practice in rush hour takes at least twenty minutes, plus extra time to pick up the two other kids in our car pool if I happen to be driving. I don't usually drive both days, but I share that responsibility with the other parents in our car pool. But even if I'm not driving, I have to feed her by about 5:00 p.m., which is much earlier than my husband comes home and earlier than any of us is actually hungry. She often gets leftovers or a sandwich because whatever I am cooking isn't ready yet.

I still often cook a meal on Tuesday, but Melanie is not there for it. On Thursday, Aaron has art class from 4:00 to 6:00 p.m. at a location fifteen minutes in the opposite direction of soccer practice. That's right; one kid's class ends at the same time the other's practice begins, in locations at least a half-hour's drive apart. Thank God for car pools (and some nights, McDonald's).

Why do I choose to do this? Because even though Thursday is a soccer practice night, it's also the night of the art class that my son wanted to take. This is the only class or activity he is in. And during other seasons, soccer practice has been on other nights. Thankfully, my neighbor's child also wanted to take the art class, so I knew I could carpool. For me, a simpler lifestyle doesn't mean avoiding extracurricular activities, it means limited activities and limiting the number of evenings per week that we have obligations. It also means I don't sign the kids up for anything unless there's car-pool potential. There are some Thursdays I am in the car from 3:45 p.m. to 8:15 p.m. but others when I only drive one leg of the art class car pool, and so I'm back home by 4:15.

Sometimes we have dinner in the car; other times I make something in the Crock-Pot and it's ready whenever we get home. Sometimes the kids do their homework in the car. So, even though Thursdays don't necessarily work well, that doesn't mean we abandon the idea of having meals together.

And I chose to have one night of my week look like this, not every night. Sabbath Simplicity is about a rhythm: if we have one night like this, we deliberately block out other nights each week when we are home and eat together as a family, around the table, not in the minivan.

What does dinnertime look like at your house? Maybe you and your spouse both work late, so the kids get fed early at the sitter's, and you're too tired to cook so you just grab something on the way home. Maybe you know your husband won't get home until after 7:00 p.m. so you give your toddlers macaroni and cheese (or scrambled eggs, a favorite at our house) at 5:00 p.m. Maybe you've given up on cooking because you're tired of hearing "Yuck! What is this?" from your kids when you put a meal on the table that you labored over.

I talked to parents who have several kids, each in more than one sport or activity, who said they usually eat fast food on their way from one game or practice to another—several nights a week. "If baseball gets rained out, it's nice; we get a break," said one mom. "But we still don't really have a family meal; half the time I don't have groceries in the house to make dinner, because we usually eat fast food. So then I've got to throw together sandwiches or we end up going out anyway. Family meals are a nice idea but not very realistic."

Don't let this happen to you! Even if you think you can't totally eliminate hurry from your life, you can plan to have a break from hurry for an hour a day: for dinner. If your children are still too young for sports, decide ahead of time what you are willing to give up in order to have them play baseball or other weeknight sports.

Not Just Food

Shared meals are not just about food, they're also about conversation. They offer an oppportunity to ask your kids about their day. We often ask the question, "What was the highlight of your day?" It's more specific than just "How was your day?" because it asks kids to recall a specific incident. You can also ask them if they had a "lowlight"—a challenge or difficulty. If you make this a regular practice, kids will come to expect it and will come to meals ready to share their thoughts.

Pastor and author Randy Frazee says having a family meal is an important ritual. He writes: "We haven't been taught the long-term value of sharing a meal and conversation at dusk; most people, therefore, believe that shoving a high-calorie, processed fast food item down our throats while riding in a seven-passenger vehicle accomplishes the same end. It doesn't. We were born with the need to unpack our day within a circle of people who know us and deeply care about us. When we exchange this kind of simple existence for a motion-obsessed existence— which takes lots of discretionary money to pull off—new evils and new illnesses are birthed in our homes and in our bodies. Simply put, when our relationship time is unbalanced, life doesn't work."[2]

More important than what you ask around the table, though, is how you listen. Force yourself to slow down as you listen, and avoid lecturing or telling kids what they ought to have done. Don't interrupt them. Teach them about respectful conversation by leading by example. Treat them as you'd like to be treated. If you told me about a challenge you faced today, how would you feel if I said, "Well, what you should have done was . . ."? You'd want to smack me, right? Certainly that would be an effective way for me to squash your desire to share your day with me. So don't do that to your kids, even if they say finding a worm on the sidewalk after it rained was their highlight and that your yelling at them was a lowlight. Say, "I understand" or "Tell me more about that." Use this time of sharing as a chance to ask for or to extend forgiveness, to simply listen to and delight in your kids.

Dr. Robert Billingham, professor of human development at Indiana University, says, "Sitting down together to eat is the most important activity of family life. Only reading together comes close in importance."[3]

Family meals create a rhythm to our day, and ultimately, to our life. Even if you think you cannot slow down totally, you can start by having a meal with your family just once a week. It's healthier, not only physically but also mentally. Studies have shown that kids who eat family meals and engage in conversation with adults tend to do better in school and have fewer problems. Check out this story from abcnews.com by Kate Rice on April 3, 2001:

> Teenagers who eat dinner with their families five times or more a week do better in school and are less likely to smoke, drink or use drugs than children who do so twice a week or less, according to research conducted by the National Center on Addiction and Substance Abuse at Columbia University.
>
> Younger children benefit from family dinners, too. For one thing, they have a better vocabulary, thanks to the exposure to more grown-up conversations, says Martha Marino, a dietitian for the Washington State Dairy Council and a member of the Nutrition Education Network of Washington.
>
> There are also nutritional benefits. Kids who eat with their families frequently eat healthier food—more fruits and vegetables, more dairy products—than children who eat with their families less frequently. And they take those healthy eating habits with them when they leave the house. Research shows that children who eat with their families make healthier food choices when eating out with their peers, according to Marino. They're more likely to eat breakfast, even when a parent is not there forcing them to.

Whether or not a family has dinner together is also a key measure of how well it functions. Pediatricians frequently ask families to tell them about meal times. "It's a marker," says Marino. "If a parent is organized enough to have family meals on a regular basis, that says a lot about having order in the home."[4]

Marino suggests these simple guidelines: At dinnertime, clear the table of other clutter (homework or mail). Establish a routine for starting the meal—light a candle or say grace. Turn off the phone and TV. Keep conversations positive. Make sure everyone gets a chance to talk. And share cleanup chores. Some parents find cleaning up is a good time for communicating.

Eating meals together is also a way to create space for God. Part of what it means to love God is to love others. A great way to show your kids love is to listen to them. When you ask your kids about their day and really listen, you are obeying Jesus's command to abide in him. Because abiding, he said, is about loving. "If you obey my commands, you will remain in my love," he said (John 15:10). And what command are we to obey? "My command is this: Love each other as I have loved you" (John 15:12). Putting a meal on the table, providing hospitality to your family, listening to your children—these are ways of loving. They are a way of breathing in God's presence and bringing others into his presence with you.

Breathing implies a rhythm: an inhale and an exhale. God designed us to work and rest. Family dinners can be an enjoyable transition from the workday to a time of rest. Meals are not just about nourishing our body but also our souls.

From a practical standpoint, you may feel intimidated by the idea of cooking. A meal does not have to be elaborate. Think of a meat (or other protein), a starch, and a vegetable or two. For instance, I often make this simple meal. I sauté boneless chicken breasts with a bit of chopped onion and garlic. I make rice. I microwave broccoli or frozen mixed vegetables. Chicken, rice, and veggies is a meal. A salad, especially one with meat and cheese in it, is a meal. Soup or stew with some good bread is a meal. Keep it simple. It's not rocket science.

Yesterday I spent most of the day writing. By dinnertime I was creatively tapped out. So we had bagel dogs (protein), chicken noodle soup (starch), and frozen peas (veggie). But the day before, I had cooked chicken, which means tomorrow we can have chicken potpie (leftover chicken with cream of chicken soup and veggies, topped with refrigerated crescent-roll dough).

Another easy way to cook dinner is to prepare it in the morning. Invest in a good slow cooker and a cookbook to go with it (the *Fix It and Forget It* cookbook is a good one with easy recipes). This allows you to assemble the meal in the morning, then let it cook all day while you are gone or doing other chores. I love using the Crock-Pot, because at about 4:45 p.m., a time when I am often feeling anxious about what to serve for dinner, I can simply relax and smell it cooking!

This is a great option for days when kids are coming and going at different times, because you can scoop out some soup or stew for the child who has to leave early and keep it warm until the rest of your family is ready to sit down together.

If you don't know how to cook, ask a friend who does to show you how. Not only will you learn something valuable, you will build a friendship as well. When you do cook, make double batches so that you have some leftovers. Or spend one day a month cooking a bunch of meals and freezing them (*Once-a-Month Cooking* is a book that can guide you in this process) so that each night you'll have something available.

The point is that you make something, even sandwiches, and you sit down together with your kids, ask them about their day, and listen. Give as much thought to the conversation as you do to what you put on the table. Even if you have preschoolers and you spent the whole day with them, you might be surprised at their perspective on the day.

In the summer, we often make breakfast the family meal. It's at a time when we're all home and the kids are not rushing off to school. In the evenings, we might be out playing or away from home, so dinner can be harder. Figure out what works for your family and for the season of life you're in. Experiment, but keep trying to find a way to gather around the table and listen to each other, to share a meal and share your thoughts. You'll be nourished in body and soul.

Breathing Exercise

What were meals like at your home growing up? Do you have fond memories or do you recall more strife and tension? Perhaps if they were less than idyllic, you might not feel a strong desire to bother with family meals. Talk to God about your experiences and your desire. How can you make family meals something your family will enjoy? What would you have to say no to in order to say yes to family meals? If you rarely eat together now, try for one or two days a week, then build from there.

6

humble

How can I find freedom?

To practice simplicity, do you have to move to the country? Do you have to eat organic foods and wear only natural fabrics? Is it possible to live a simple life in the midst of a big city? Can you embrace the Sabbath Simplicity lifestyle in an urban environment?

Elise and her husband believe it's not only possible, but that the city is, for them, the place where it is easiest to live simply in a way that reflects their values and ideals.

Elise was a banker. She started right out of college and worked her way up the ladder at a large downtown bank. She loved her job and was good at it—successful and well-respected. She earned a very good salary but lived frugally, being careful to keep her expenses low, at first out of necessity.

"When I first got out of college, I felt financially burdened because I had a lot of student loans I had to pay
off," Elise recalls. "But I felt really proud of myself for
paying them off."

She'd known her husband since college, but they didn't
start dating until about ten years after graduation. Both
were well-established in their careers by the time they
married about two years later.

They bought a small condo and lived simply. They took
public transportation most of the time. Their primary focus
was work, where they both would put in long days. Elise
was at her desk by 7:30 a.m. most days and was there until
6:00 p.m. and as late as 9:00 p.m. a couple of days a week.
"That was the cultural expectation," she says.

As they advanced in their careers, however, they chose
not to advance their lifestyle. "Since I was in finance, I
looked at things from a financial model," Elise says. "I
looked at our fixed expenses and variable expenses. My
goal has always been to keep my fixed expenses as low as
possible. So we stayed in that small condo for three years,
even though people asked us why we didn't want to get
something with a bit more space."

Not long after they were married, a friend at church
approached them. He was building three-flat condo
homes in an area that was being revitalized. It was a
block or two from some public housing high-rises that
were slowly being torn down and emptied. The residents
were being moved to more integrated housing, some of
it on their street. A block or two in the other direction, a
once rather seedy area was being revamped with stores
like Banana Republic and the Gap. The building was on a
quiet, tree-lined street. The neighborhood, however, was
still seen by most people as improving but not exactly a
hot location.

In fact, this would be one of several buildings in the area that was part of a public housing reform project. One of the units in their building would be owned by the Chicago Housing Authority and occupied by tenants who had formerly lived in a public housing high-rise, their rent subsidized by the city as part of a welfare program.

Elise and Dan thought it over, knowing that it would be a bit of a gamble: Would the social experiment work? Would their condo increase in value? Finally, they decided to buy the condo, in part because it was affordable, and they wanted to keep their payments about the same as they had been on their smaller condo. The choice also reflected their values.

"It's one thing to say you think integrated housing is a good idea, but if you really think that, you have to be willing to invest in it and live there," Elise says. "The family that used to live in public housing and now lives in our building is great. They have a son who plays with my son. They gave us a baby gift when my daughter was born. They're just a part of the neighborhood."

Jesus invites us to be gentle and humble. For Elise and Dan, that means being willing to associate with and befriend people from whom society often insulates us.

When Elise had her first child, she took a three-month maternity leave, which actually stretched into almost four months because she was having trouble finding a nanny. But the bank wanted her back, and as hard as it was to leave her young son in someone else's care, she and her husband weren't ready to give up her salary.

"When we bought this place, either one of us could afford it on our salary," Elise says. "Our cost of living was reasonable. I've always been very careful about keeping my fixed expenses low. Even before I had children, I never wanted to get myself into a high-powered lifestyle that would require me to stay in my job if I wanted to do something else. But when my son was born, I wasn't ready to quit yet. I went back to work, and we saved my salary."

Living in the city, neither Elise or Dan had long, stressful commutes. They lived a block or two from the elevated train station that could get them to work in about fifteen minutes. Because they lived in a condo, they did not have to spend time doing yard work or maintenance on their home, which can be time-consuming, expensive, and stressful. Because the home was new, home improvement projects were unnecessary. They didn't have to spend their weekends shopping at Home Depot or trying to install a new garbage disposal.

Elise loved her job but sometimes missed her little son when she was away at work. The arrangement had seemed at the time to be the best for their family. The nanny seemed to be responsible and competent. Then one day, a neighbor called.

The neighbor had been looking out the window when the nanny wheeled Elise's baby out in his stroller. She went out their locked front gate, then apparently realized she had forgotten something in the house. Rather than take the baby out of the stroller and back up the one and a half flights of stairs to the condo, she left him sitting in his stroller, on the sidewalk, outside the front gate. Alone.

Concerned, the neighbor went out and stood near the stroller, keeping an eye on the six-month-old baby until the nanny returned more than five minutes later.

The neighbor called Elise that night just to let her know that her nanny might not be as responsible as she had thought.

"It was a Friday," Elise recalled. "Over the weekend, we agonized over what to do. Except for this, we liked this nanny. She had done a good job. I didn't know what to do.

There's this complexity of the relationship you have with a nanny: you want them to love your child; it's almost like they are family. But they are not; they are an employee. Still, we had entrusted our son to her. I remember as we talked about it, Dan for the first time asked me, 'Would you be open to staying home?' But it wasn't easy. We just kept saying, What do we do now? It was awful."

They decided to fire the nanny. Before doing so, they called Dan's parents, who live about an hour away from them, and asked if they'd be willing to help take care of their grandson, and they graciously agreed. But Elise knew she couldn't rely on family who had to drive an hour each way to care for her baby every day as a long-term solution.

"I realized I needed to cut back at work," she says. She investigated being able to work from home two days a week, an arrangement other employees at the bank had. At first, she thought she'd have to take a cut in pay, but she found she could keep her full-time job by working three days at the bank and two days at home.

She found a new nanny, who could work three and a half days a week—the three Elise was away and a half day when she was home, so that Elise could work from home. She still had to keep tabs on her clients, which she did by phone, even taking her cell phone to the park when she took her son there.

The new nanny "was wonderful," Elise says. "If she had been able to stay, things might have unfolded differently." Unfortunately, the nanny's family situation changed and she had to quit. Elise found yet another nanny, this one for four days a week.

While the arrangement worked, trying to keep up with phone messages and emails the day the nanny wasn't there was rather difficult. "Also, things started shifting at work, and I realized, career-wise, I needed to make a move," Elise says. "I actually got a nice job offer from another bank at that time. But I didn't know if that was the right move. I remember sitting outside one day, thinking about how my life would unfold. I knew I wanted to get pregnant again, and since I was thirty-seven, I didn't want to put that off for very long. I didn't want to take on a new job and try to give that attention if I was going to be having another baby. I realized I was probably going to leave my job."

She didn't leave right away though. The idea of losing her income was a bit scary for them, she remembers. Even though they were living on one salary and saving the other, both of them liked having the safety net of the other's job. They liked being able to put money away every month.

However, the choices they had made to live simply and not beyond their means made it easier for Elise to follow her heart. Because they had lived frugally for the first several years of their marriage, they were able to pay off the mortgage on the condo and set aside some savings as a cushion.

It came down to the fact, "I wanted time alone with my firstborn," she says. She quit five months before her daughter was born, giving her some precious time with her little boy before his sister was born.

Elise's children are now one and three years old, and she is at home full-time with them. Having done the working mom drill of getting up and dressed and out the door at dawn, trying to manage a high-powered job and caring for her children, she sees this season of motherhood "as the most self-indulgent time of my life. We don't have to hurry. We can stay in our pajamas all morning if we want."

While he was apprehensive at first about losing Elise's income, Dan sees the incalculable value of having their children spend these early years with their mom. He also appreciates that she can take care of small details that used to eat up their weekends, things such as getting the oil changed in the car or doing the grocery shopping.

Her son now goes to preschool two mornings a week, giving her time alone with her daughter. "Dan takes him to school, so I only have to pick him up," Elise says, which means she doesn't have to get her daughter up and dressed to take her son to school. They have family memberships at many of the museums in the city, which are close to their home, so it's not unusual for her to take the kids to a museum or the aquarium for an hour or two in the morning and then come home for lunch and naps.

Because her husband can take the train to work, they have only one car, an eight-year-old Ford Escort. If they didn't live in the city, they would likely need a second car, which would increase their cost of living in gas, car payments, and insurance. "We could afford a nicer car, but we've chosen not to," Elise says.

She's in a playgroup with some of her more affluent neighbors, who drive expensive cars and live a different lifestyle than she has chosen. "It's a constant battle. I think most of my peers assume we just don't have much money. Part of me wants to tell them that I could afford to drive a car like they have," she admits. "It's like a spiritual battle. I don't need to tell them that I'm living below my means; I don't need to defend myself or my choices. But part of me wants to."

Their car is another part of how Elise and Dan practice simplicity—driving a modest car that doesn't use much fuel, doesn't have high insurance rates, and best of all, is paid for. "We're thinking about replacing the car, because a Ford Escort is a bit small for a family of four. But the other day, I had to park, and I pulled into this little spot between two big SUVs and it struck me: if I had a bigger car or an SUV, I wouldn't be able to park it so easily."

We can move toward simplicity when we take a long-term view and make choices thoughtfully. Elise and Dan could afford a more expensive house, a more luxurious car. They could choose to move to a bigger house in the suburbs with a big yard to maintain, bigger property taxes to pay, and longer commutes. They could choose to both work and have more disposable income. Yet by choosing a humbler lifestyle, they have embraced simplicity, and with it, a sense of freedom.

"Because we have no debt and very low fixed expenses, we can respond generously when we hear about someone in need, through our church or whatever," Elise says. "I don't feel weighed down by anything that forces me to stay on the same track."

Breathing Exercise

How does where you live affect your ability to practice simplicity? Whether you live in the country, the city, or somewhere in between, what can you learn from Elise's story? How do the choices of external things like the car you drive and the size of your home affect your ability to keep life simple?

Living Your Values

Elise's story reminds us that a key aspect of simplicity is living your values. If you say that you value people over stuff, if you say that you value helping the poor, if you say you want to spend time with your family but you don't arrange the details of your life to be able to do those things, you create an inner anxiety for yourself. Thoreau wrote, "Your priorities are what you do." Elise and Dan have made lifestyle choices that allow them to live out their priorities. Their life is outwardly simple but also inwardly simple, because there is a congruency between the way they would "like to" live and the way they actually are living.

If I say I would "like to" spend time alone with God, but I don't actually do it, there's this disconnect, this duplicity, in my heart. If we say our kids are a priority but we spend more time shopping than with them, then we are fooling ourselves. When we actually take steps to live out the things we say that we value, we are moving toward simplicity.

If you find a dichotomy between the way you say you would "like to" live and the way you are actually living, you have two choices. You can change the way you live, or you can get more honest about what you really value. For example, I value being comfortable. I don't think that's particularly admirable, but it's the truth. When God pushes me out of my comfort zone, I don't like it. But over time, I have begun to let go of needing to be comfortable quite so much. I am moving toward saying, "I value being with you, God, even if you put me in uncomfortable situations, even if you put me in challenging situations."

I've talked to many people who did not mean to get into debt; they just decided to fix up the house or replace the car and sort of found themselves with credit card bills that are taking a long time to pay off. They are not sure how they got into the situation, but it's causing a lot of stress.

You don't have to duplicate the lifestyle that Elise and Dan have chosen in order to live out those same values. But I would urge you to follow their example in listening to what God is inviting *you* to do. Part of the freedom of simplicity comes from thinking through all the implications of your financial choices.

A Gentle Life

Jesus says he is gentle, and he invites us to learn from him. What exactly does that mean? That he will gently teach us or that he will teach us to be gentle?

Both, of course. Jesus is strong but also loving. He will not force us to come to him, but he always stands inviting us to do so. When we come, he gently teaches us about gentleness. He humbly offers us guidance on how to live a humble life.

Humility is not a very popular attribute in our society. Gentleness is even less so.

We live in a violent world, and I'm not just talking about drive-by shootings and wars in the Middle East.

Much of the violence in our lives, and hence, the stress, comes from our effort to win and to control. We want to control our kids in three easy steps. We want to make our spouse give us what we want. We want to look good and feel good, and we get bummed if our friends look and feel better than we do.

We live competitively, whether we are trying to move up the career ladder at work, fight for a spot for our child at the "right" preschool, or finally be able to afford a house in the "right" neighborhood. It's hard to live simply when we are always striving to beat everyone else. It's hard to slow down when we are afraid everyone else will get ahead of us if we do.

Success and gentleness seem to be at odds. "A 'successful' life has become a violent enterprise," writes Wayne Muller. "We make war on our bodies, pushing them beyond their limits; war on our children, because we cannot find enough time to be with them when they are hurt and afraid, and need our company; war on our spirit, because we are too preoccupied to listen to the quiet voices that seek to nourish and refresh us; war on our communities, because we are fearfully protecting what we have, and do not feel safe enough to be kind and generous; war on the earth, because we cannot take the time to place our feet on the ground and allow it to feed us, to taste its blessings and give thanks."[1]

Eliminating Worry

As I have explored simplicity, I find that it is not just about slowing down and eliminating hurry. I find it helps if we can also eliminate worry. When Elise decided to stay home with her children, she eliminated the worry of whether someone else would do a good job caring for them. She could easily have chosen to add the worry of whether they could make ends meet on one income, but she chose to trust.

Trust is a huge part of simplicity. If you have trouble trusting God or even other people, you'll need to spend some time working on that before you can really embrace the practice of simplicity. Having a singular focus on Christ—the heart of simplicity—is impossible if you don't really trust him.

I know I've often found myself longing for a simpler life but have not been willing to take my eyes off my problems and challenges. That puts me back to double-mindedness again, losing my focus.

In chapter 4, we looked at Jesus's teaching on storing up treasures in heaven and how simplicity involves having a "single eye." What distracts us? What pulls our focus away from Christ? Fear. Jesus acknowledges this in Matthew 6: "Therefore, I tell you, do not worry about your life, what you will eat or drink; or about your body, what you will wear" (v. 25).

Ruthlessly eliminate worry. What would that look like?

Well, what do you worry about? You can't obey Jesus's direction to not worry unless you know what it is you're worried about.

I don't like to admit it, but a lot of what I worry about is whether people like me, whether I fit in. I also worry about the things Jesus mentioned, things like food and clothing. I worry about my career, my husband's career. Will I sell the next magazine article? Will I get a contract for the book? Will we earn enough to pay our expenses this year?

Genuine Humility

Humility means not thinking too highly of yourself. It means not thinking that your hard work (or your husband's) is the only thing that provides the basic necessities for your family. God provides for us spiritually, but he also makes our labor fruitful to provide food and shelter.

Humility means not living beyond our means. Why do we overspend? Mostly, we want to have certain things (from new shoes to a bigger house) that we think will make us look better, more successful, more attractive to others. Humility says, I don't need to impress other people; I'm not focused on looking important or even successful. If we say we value people more than stuff, then we can begin to trust God enough to let go of our addiction to stuff and live the value of loving people.

If I am genuinely humble, success and its trappings are less important to me. I want to be that humble, but I have a long way to go. What moves me toward humility? Taking Jesus's easy yoke, putting my focus on him instead of on myself and how other people see me. And if I am loved by someone who is humble and gentle, who invites me to come to him, who is a safe refuge for my soul, then I am okay with not having all the "stuff" that I think might raise other people's opinions of me. Because if I am focusing on him, I know that he loves me deeply, and it doesn't matter whether other people are impressed by me. How could I live more humbly and gently? Let go of image management, and come to Jesus.

The phrase "gentle and humble" in Matthew 11:29 is translated in the King James Version as "meek and lowly." Perhaps because of this, I used to have a hard time with this particular verse. I didn't want to be meek and lowly. That sounded a lot like a description of a doormat.

But Jesus had this strange kind of gentleness—it was really strength. *Meek* is a word we don't really use anymore, because we think it means "weak." While it has connotations of submissiveness, a person who is meek endures difficulty or persecution with patience. Jesus did this. He responded with humility, but he seemed to move through his life with an inner conviction, an inner strength and purpose. He responded to people gently, humbly, but thoughtfully. As a friend of mine noted when she first started reading the Bible: "That Jesus, he's pretty clever."

Jesus didn't have a secretary telling him his agenda each day. He didn't have spin doctors or speech writers. People came into his path, and he was mindful and present enough to see what they really needed—a word of truth, a healing touch, or just his attention. He didn't get pulled in a million directions, despite the efforts of a lot of people to do just that.

He responded to each person without trying to impose his agenda, noticing what they really needed (not necessarily what they said or thought they needed). That is real humility: knowing everything in the universe, literally, and never acting like a know-it-all.

Jesus . . . Interrupted

We can learn a lot about how to live like Jesus did by seeing how he handled interruptions. Look at Mark 5:21–43. Jesus, after a busy day of ministry, including a rather unpopular interaction between some demons and swine, sails across a lake to get away from the crowds, only to be greeted (read: interrupted) by another large group of people. Perhaps he had planned to take a break, but he doesn't get the chance. As he's speaking to this new crowd, Jairus, a synagogue ruler, comes and asks him to heal his daughter. He essentially interrupts Jesus's teaching. The text says Jairus "fell at his feet," begging Jesus to come to his home. Outwardly, that seems rather humble. How pure were Jairus's motives? We don't know. After all, the religious leaders were not all that enamored with Jesus and his teachings.

Jesus's response is interesting. He doesn't tell Jairus, "Go away, I'm too busy for you." Despite the fact that the religious leaders had been extremely critical of Jesus, and he in turn had taken many of them to task for hypocrisy, he doesn't judge Jairus. He responds gently, humbly, lovingly. He's still willing to see each person as an individual. He sees this interruption as an opportunity for ministry. And not just his healing ministry.

On his way to heal Jairus's daughter, a woman tries to pickpocket a healing from Jesus. (Interrupted again!)

Women in that culture were second-class citizens. The text says this woman had suffered from bleeding for many years. A woman with this kind of reproductive health issue was even further down in the pecking order. This woman was also desperate, and she had been desperate for far longer than Jairus. Up until then, Jairus probably felt pretty self-sufficient. People looked up to him. He would be considered by many to be a man of faith, a role model. In that culture, he would have been considered much more important and more righteous and religious than the woman. Most likely, he would have considered himself that way as well.

The text says the woman came up in the crowd and touched the edge of Jesus's robe. This was a tremendous act of faith; she was, by her actions, affirming her belief that this was not just a miracle-worker or rabbi but the Messiah, who had "healing in his wings."

Jesus stops. "Who touched me?" he asks as the crowd presses and surges around him. His "helpful" disciples almost laugh. "Jesus, you're getting touched all the time; don't pay any attention. C'mon Jesus, let's go heal the Pharisee's daughter; it will be good PR. The religious types are kind of annoyed with you, so maybe this healing will improve your image with them."

But Jesus is not interested in improving his image or going for the most noteworthy miracle. He insists on stopping. Meanwhile, this woman is amazed because she can feel in her body that she's been healed. But she's also terrified. By Jewish law, she would be considered "unclean" and had been so for twelve years. For an unclean person to touch a rabbi was criminal. What kind of self-esteem would you expect this woman to have, being told she's "unclean" for most of her adult life? Humble doesn't even begin to describe it. And yet she is incredibly courageous. But when she realizes she's been found out, she is undone.

Jesus could have healed her quietly. He knew someone had touched him; I'm guessing he even knew who it was and everything she had been through. He could have let it go and saved the woman any embarrassment. Wouldn't that have been the gentlest thing? Why does he interrupt his interaction with Jairus to talk to this woman?

Because he saw interruptions as an opportunity for ministry. He didn't see himself as too important to speak a word of loving affirmation to a person society saw as insignificant, undesirable, unclean. He was mindful of the fact that his mission was to proclaim the good news that the kingdom of God is for everyone, not just people who appear to have it all together. He wanted to publicly affirm that to this woman. But he also wanted to teach the rest of the crowd, including Jairus, that truth as well.

So he stops. The Bible doesn't say it, but I'll bet Jairus was a bit ticked off. He might have been tempted to think: *Doesn't this country rabbi know who I am? Why does he delay?* And when the woman falls before them, realizing she's been found out, what do you think Jairus is thinking? In a small town like this one, everyone probably knew this woman. Pity was probably not Jairus's first response. I'm thinking annoyance or even disgust would be more like it. I can imagine him thinking, *The nerve of this woman— touching the rabbi, interrupting us.* Not exactly humble thoughts.

Jesus saw this interruption as an opportunity to proclaim the good news, not just to the woman, but to Jairus as well. When she realizes she's been found out, the woman does the same thing Jairus did: she "fell at his feet." I'm pretty sure her humility was not false. It may, however, have been mixed with a bit of terror.

First, Jesus says to the woman, "Daughter, your faith has healed you." He doesn't call her "unclean woman." He treats her gently: "Daughter." To the outcast, he says, "You are now part of my family."

What is Jairus thinking about this? Certainly, his thoughts and emotions are swirling. "Daughter? What about *my* daughter?" Then look at what happens. As Jesus is speaking to the woman (something most rabbis would never do, let alone do in the way Jesus did), word comes that Jairus's daughter has died. The text doesn't tell us what Jairus said or did. But we can assume that he was upset, based on Jesus's words.

"Don't be afraid; just have faith," he says to Jairus. And they both look at the woman, the one who should have been afraid but wasn't. The one kneeling on the ground thinking she'd be struck dead for her boldness, her chutzpah, and instead finding herself blessed beyond what she could ever hope or imagine. The one whose faith, Jesus had just proclaimed, had healed her. The one Jesus called "daughter." She's just as much a daughter as the child of an "important" man, just as loved. Jesus tells Jairus, through both words and actions: "Don't be afraid. Just have faith, like this unclean woman, like this person you don't think even matters. Don't despise her. Aspire to be like her." And now it's Jairus who is undone.

Jesus lived in a way that allowed him to see teachable moments and seize upon them. His mission was to heal the sick and proclaim the good news. So although he was interrupted, it didn't take him from his task. It allowed him to fulfill his mission.

Jesus was often interrupted by people who wanted something from him. Can you relate? My life often feels like a series of interruptions. Reacting to those often makes me feel hurried and bothered. I may not say it, but secretly I think I'm too important to deal with this. Jesus, on the other hand, was not hurried. He didn't ignore the needs of people, but he took time to discern what their real needs were. Jairus needed to have his daughter healed, but he also needed to learn about humility, to learn about how God really sees people. He needed a healing of his heart. And Jesus graciously provided both.

Given the fact that Jesus walked our planet for about thirty-three years—and only three of those in his "official" ministry—you'd think he'd have been tempted to be hurried. He had a difficult mission and not a lot of time to accomplish it. Jesus, faced with what he knew would be a short-term assignment, particularly from his eternal perspective, certainly worked hard. The Gospel writers, especially Matthew and Mark, repeatedly use words like "immediately," or give a sense that Jesus moved through his full days in a purposeful way.

Jesus's life was busy but simple. He did a lot, but he didn't seem to hurry. You can search the Gospels and never find a verse that says, "And lo, the Lord Jesus was hurried." In fact, when other people tried to get him to hurry, he refused. He gently reproved Martha for her hustle and bustle, for being worried and distracted. He corrected his disciples when they tried to convince some women and children that Jesus was too busy to greet them. Jesus was never in a hurry. He was fully present with people, whether they were religious leaders or lepers. He responded gently to the inevitable interruptions of life.

Do you see interruptions as an opportunity for ministry? Are you mindful and unhurried enough to discern what people really need and whether you can give it to them? Are you humble enough to listen to what is really going on before you tell them how to fix themselves? I sometimes have to admit that my frustration with interruptions is mostly about my desire to be in control.

If I want to live a life of Sabbath Simplicity, Jesus is a good role model. He was clear on his mission, so he was able to see that sometimes the interruptions of life were a part of his mission.

Some days, interruptions annoy me more than others. The longer my "to-do" list is, the more I am rattled by other people wanting me to do something for them, something that is not on the list.

I've found that it is easier to see interruptions as opportunities to love other people if I keep my own agenda very short. Not that I ignore my own needs, not at all. But I seriously evaluate everything on the list and make sure it really needs to be done.

I had a friend who would mop her kitchen floor about five times a day. (Why, I'm not sure. I'm not a therapist.) She would get annoyed (as would anyone) when, as she was scrubbing the floor on her hands and knees, her toddler would climb onto her calves (ouch!) and then try to climb onto her back. But why was she cleaning the floor five times a day? Because it got messy that often? Well, yes, of course it did. She had two preschoolers. But wouldn't her life have been less frustrating if she had decided to shorten her list? To tell herself that regardless of how messy it got, she would just clean it completely once at the end of the day, after the children were in bed? A little more mess, perhaps, but a lot less frustration. This method would also have given the toddler fewer opportunities to use her for a jungle gym when she really didn't want to be one. And it would have given her time to just play and snuggle on the floor with her toddler, which was what her child needed and wanted.

If you have a shorter list, you have more space for interruptions. If you keep the list in line with your mission as a mom, you'll have a different perspective on those interruptions. You'll be able to respond to your child's needs rather than just reacting in anger or frustration.

If you're trying to straighten up the house or cook dinner and your kids are whining or hanging on your leg or asking you a million questions, take a deep breath. Remember that part of your mission is to love them and raise them into responsible, caring adults. If I'm cooking dinner to nourish their bodies but not willing to listen to their questions or problems even for a few seconds—in other words, to nourish their souls—have I accomplished my mission?

Breathing Exercise

Think about a time recently when you were interrupted. How did you feel? How did you react? Take several slow, deep breaths. How are you feeling now about the way you handled that situation? Sit and breathe and reflect on whatever comes to mind. If you mishandled the situation, simply let it go. Don't wallow in guilt or regret. Now imagine yourself back in that situation. Imagine how Jesus would react to that kind of interruption. This time, imagine yourself responding in a mindful way, perhaps imitating Jesus's response. Pray that God will bring some interruptions your way so you can practice what you have learned.

Fulfilling a Mission

Jesus's humility flowed out of his awareness that he was not setting the agenda for his life but rather doing the work that his Father had called him to do.

What is God calling you to do? If you are simply being obedient, you will find it easier to be humble. Obedience and humility are two sides of the same coin.

If you want to follow Jesus and take on his yoke, you can approach it the hard way, by just trying really hard to act humble. But as that old country song goes, "Oh Lord, it's hard to be humble, when you're perfect in every way."

Just trying to appear humble is not humility. It's image management. The easy way to be humble is by asking God, "What are you calling me to do?" and then humbly obeying him. The Bible says God "saved us and called us to a holy life—not because of anything we have done but because of his own purpose and grace" (2 Tim. 1:9).

Humility doesn't mean pretending you are worthless or thinking you can't do anything. It's just the opposite. You can do a lot, and God is calling you to do it. When you move forward in obedience, you can accomplish whatever God has asked you to do.

Paul, in his letter to the church at Rome, prefaces his teaching on spiritual gifts (which is really about fulfilling your specific mission) by saying, "Do not think of yourself more highly than you ought, but rather think of yourself with sober judgment, in accordance with the measure of faith God has given you" (Rom. 12:3).

Sober judgment does not mean to put yourself down; it does not mean having false humility, which is worse than no humility at all. It means having a realistic view of yourself but also believing that God could call you to something bigger than yourself, something he deems important, whether it's caring for your children, tending a home, running a business, serving in your church, or just being kind to your annoying neighbors.

Discerning your calling begins with listening. Parker Palmer writes: "Vocation does not come from willfulness. It comes from listening. I must listen to my life and try to understand what it is truly about—quite apart from what I would like it to be about—or my life will never represent anything real in the world, no matter how earnest my intentions."[2]

The only way we can do that kind of deep listening is to slow the pace of our lives. We cannot listen in a hurry.

A few years ago, after a lot of prayer and thought, I wrote this mission statement about my ministry: "To shepherd others toward deeper devotion to Christ through clear and compelling words."

Having that mission in front of me helps me to discern what I should say yes and no to. It helps stave off that "focus creep" that can easily plague my heart.

I have found that this mission applies not only to my writing and teaching but also to my parenting and interaction with my neighbors. I want my words to build up my friends, to point them toward God's grace. I want to be the same person at PTA that I am when I am leading a church retreat. Not that I preach at PTA meetings but that I treat others as Jesus would treat them. If I disagree with someone, do I express it in a loving way? I can be very opinionated. Do I state my opinions in a gentle way, in a way that glorifies Christ? Keeping my mission clear helps me to do that.

Shepherding others doesn't mean shepherding everyone all the time. I often have to say no to speaking requests or opportunities to serve at church so that I can shepherd my kids.

We mothers have been told, "You are raising the future leaders of our country, our churches, etc." When my daughter was born and I was agonizing over my transition from highly visible career woman to work-from-home mom, I would often cringe when people asked, "So what do you do?"

My friend Sue (who worked in a day-care center and had seen firsthand what a key role parents play in their kids' lives) suggested I boldly reply, "I'm raising a warrior for Christ. And what do *you* do?"

Is God calling you to raise a warrior for Christ? That may be the case. Does that make you feel proud? It makes me feel humbled that God would give me such an important job.

As I embrace my mission, I sometimes feel overwhelmed by it. I think I better not screw up. Unfortunately, I have sometimes fooled myself into thinking that getting it right means doing a lot, at a rapid pace, so I can fit it all in.

But what kind of warped thinking is that? If I want to get it right, shouldn't I slow down? Shouldn't I focus on my priorities? Shouldn't I try to *simplify*?

If I want to show the love of Christ to my family, don't I need to set aside some time to be with Christ and soak in his love so I can then share that love? If I am running around saying yes to all kinds of other things and pouring myself out for other people, I could easily end up depleted. How will I share the love of God with my family if my heart is depleted? I wouldn't intentionally give strangers my best self and my family the leftovers, but if I'm not careful, that can happen.

Sometimes the best thing you can do for your kids is to say no to the needs of others, set aside some time to be alone with God, and pace yourself so that your family gets your best. On the other hand, sometimes saying yes to outside interests, whether they are employment, ministry, or just a friendship that feeds your soul, can give you energy and renewal that will help you be a better mom.

The key is listening and paying attention. Before saying yes or no to anything, ask yourself whether it will help or hinder you in your mission.

Breathing Exercise

Do you have a personal mission statement or a clear idea of what God is calling you to do? Spend some time writing down the things you do each day. How are they connected? What is the goal of your efforts as a parent, friend, worker?

Spend some time praying about this. Spend time in silence, listening for God's direction. Where do you sense God telling you to focus your efforts?

If you haven't before, craft a personal mission statement. Keep it brief, a sentence or two. Begin to think about the many things you do and ask yourself how these things fit in with your mission. If they don't fit, why are you doing them?

part four

the promise

And you will find rest
for your souls

7

rested

How can I keep Sabbath?

Patti and her husband, Bruce, have four children, ages nine, seven, five, and three. They find it challenging to keep their lives at a manageable pace. It has taken intentionality and effort on both of their parts to keep things sane.

Bruce works many hours, often not making it home for dinner. When I first met her, Patti was volunteering about twenty hours a week managing a team in the mentoring ministry at her church. With the equivalent of a part-time job and four children, Patti has been careful about not getting sucked into the overscheduling that is endemic in her suburban culture.

"There have always been definite limits," she says. "The kids can do just one sport at a time." Currently, only her oldest two are participating in park district sport programs (no travel teams or heavy time commitments), and they don't take any other classes or activities.

About two years ago, Patti began a journey to simplify and slow her life even more. She was in a class that I taught, where we discussed the idea of Sabbath-keeping as a spiritual practice. Patti was intrigued by what she was reading and discussing in class.

As we read Marjorie Thompson's book *Soul Feast*, these words on Sabbath resonated deeply with Patti: "The Sabbath command is especially relevant to contemporary life. How difficult it is for people in our achievement- and production-obsessed culture to rest. Keeping the Sabbath means trusting God to be God, recognizing that we are not indispensable. When we refuse to take a single day a week for genuine refreshment and rest, we try to outdo even God! In the light of God's rest, our anxious, compulsive activities may be exposed as little more than efforts to stay in control, or to fabricate life's meaning out of constant activity."[1]

In class, we talked a lot about how the pace of our lives affected the way we related to God. We talked about spiritual practices and how they create space for God, but only if they are not "add-ons" to a hurried life.

Patti talked to Bruce about the things she was learning and reading and suggested they try clearing out their Sunday schedules to have a day of rest.

"Before we made the change, Sunday was church in the morning, but then the rest of it was like any other day. We focused on our agenda: housework, home-improvement projects, shopping, running errands, even going to the mall. It looked just like Saturday," she says.

How can you "do Sabbath" with four young children (who at the time were seven and younger)? Patti believes it's actually easier when the kids are younger and not tempted to go out with friends or be involved in too many outside activities.

"We simply eliminated work from that day," she says. "No housework, no laundry. No projects, which tended to stress us out. I've met people who say, 'No way; I can't do this with young children.' I would say that's exactly the time you should do it."

Sabbath is not about rules. In part it's about relaxing and not doing chores or errands, but it is more than that. It's about honoring and strengthening connections: to each other and to God. Because their children are small, Patti and her husband often find that the most loving thing they can do is to talk to and play with their children rather than focusing on the grown-up work they normally have to do. Through the simple act of paying attention to their children, they model what God is like: a loving Father who is interested in simply being with us, who is not too busy to listen and spend time with us.

How It Plays Out

These days, Sundays at Patti's house look something like this: the family goes to 9:00 a.m. church service, where the kids attend a terrific Sunday school program and Patti and Bruce can worship.

In nice weather, they sometimes bring a picnic to church and have lunch on the grounds. Other times they enjoy a walk on the path that goes through the church campus. They do so at a leisurely pace, noticing bugs, leaves, and other things in nature. As they notice these things, they talk about the God who made them. They do not hurry. They live close enough to church that when the weather is good, they walk from home to church.

"We look for God together," Patti explains. "We talk about what the kids learned at church and about what we see in creation. We pray."

Other times they have a big breakfast at home after church. "I don't love to cook, so sometimes we go out for breakfast," Patti admits. "If we have breakfast at home, I let the kids help. I let them flip pancakes. It gets a little messy, but it's fun."

After that, they simply have some downtime. Sometimes the whole family will nap. The kids play together, and sometimes the family will watch sports on television.

Often Sunday is the day for what they call a "family meeting." The content of this varies widely. "Sometimes it's about problem solving," Patti says. "Other times, it's a time where we try to get the kids thinking about God. I want to listen to where they are at spiritually. Once I had them draw our neighborhood, and then we prayed for our neighbors."

On occasion, these meetings involve creative family devotions. "We once brainstormed on the question, 'What makes God smile?'" Patti says. "At Easter, we drew pictures about each day of Holy Week as we read stories from the Bible."

An important caveat about these family meetings: when they first started, Patti and Bruce did not expect their youngest two kids (ages one and three at the time) to sit still. "The older ones got into it; they had their special spot to sit and things they wanted to talk to us about. But the younger two could move around."

In other words, be realistic. Toddlers are not going to participate at the same level as older children. But the tone you set in your home will affect even the youngest child. Also, make the meeting about *listening* to your kids, not lecturing to them.

"The kids' response to practicing Sabbath was a huge part of why we kept doing it," Patti says. "They loved it. It was amazing. I think they liked that we were available to them."

She recalls tucking in her son after they had been practicing Sabbath-keeping for a few months. As he lay in bed, he asked, "What day is it tomorrow, Mom?" When she told him it was Sunday, he said, "YESSSS! It's the Sabbath!"

Another of her children, when they had a houseguest, proudly informed the guest, "You're lucky. You get to be here for Sabbath."

Sunday night is sometimes a movie night, when the family eats popcorn and watches a movie together. The activity they share is not always the same, but the important thing is that they do it together.

Being Flexible

Learning to do Sabbath as a family has not always been easy for Patti and Bruce. Some weeks, keeping Sabbath works, but not every single week. "At first, the house would end up trashed by Monday, and I'd be angry because I had to clean it up," Patti said. "Now we're learning how to set things up, to start with a clean house on Saturday. I'm teaching the kids that they still have to be respectful and clean things up as they go. Sometimes we've had everyone help clean up after sundown on Sunday."

As appealing as a day off from chores might be, Patti has found it sometimes requires discipline. "I'd go to throw in a load of laundry, and the kids would say, 'Mom, no work on Sunday!' It's kind of funny, but they would hold us accountable."

Where has this practice taken the family? "It has given us space," Patti says. "It's a time where we are not rushing by each other, where we can be together."

While many people are amazed that Patti and Bruce are able to "do Sabbath" with four youngsters, for them it was only the beginning of a journey deeper into Sabbath Simplicity. Despite the restful Sundays, Patti found that managing a household of four young kids and working in a people-intensive ministry twenty hours a week left her feeling scattered and distracted.

"I was waking up panicky," Patti says. "I would do a breath prayer, and I'd tell myself, you need to listen. I'd just have this feeling: I'm not the 'me' I want to be. I'm scattered. I realized that when I was with my kids, I was not able to see their faces. I was thinking about ministry stuff instead of them."

Although it was unpaid, Patti's job at church was important to her. "I have teaching and strategic leadership gifts. I wanted to hang on to that," she says. She loved the positive feedback she got from others she worked with, who told her how much they appreciated her work and her impact on the church. Yet she felt God was telling her to listen, to simplify.

"I asked Bruce to tell me honestly: 'Am I a happy person? Am I joyful to be around?' Because I felt crabby all the time. In the mentoring training at church, I was teaching people how to listen, how to be attentive. I was doing that in mentoring but not to my own children. Bruce was very honest; he said that I seemed uptight and harried."

Patti realized that God was asking her to let go of her position at church to focus on her family, at least for this season. "It's hard. It's about finding worth. Is it enough just to be a mom? For a while, I was really wrestling with God. I wanted to hang on to my ministry. But now I'm realizing that being a mom *is* a ministry. I have a short season to do it right. And I'm not going to be putting my gifts aside. I'm going to be leading my family, teaching my children."

Getting to that point took some time, Patti says. For a long time, she prayed about her decision and tried to pay attention to God's leadings. "When I go to bed, I do a review of the day. I found that every day, as I thought about the events of the day, there was some point where I would feel some guilt about my kids, what I did or did not do for them."

As she prayed, God brought some images to mind, which Patti says helped her understand her mission for this season of life. "God gave me a word picture of a light. If it is spread out, it's not very bright. But if it is focused, like a laser, it can cut through steel like butter. I thought about that, about what I want my impact on my kids to be."

Another picture that came to mind was a wheel. She knew she needed to be the hub of the wheel for her family, to be the center. "Instead, I was out there on the edge, running around crazy and harried."

Still, letting go of her job was hard. "I had spent three years building this ministry," she says. "At first, I denied that there was a problem. It took awhile to acknowledge that God was asking me to give it up. I was sad; there was a grieving process. But eventually, there was also joy. I knew if God was asking me to do it, it was going to be the best thing."

Patti allowed God to do some pruning. Just because God called Patti to be at home full-time doesn't make that option the only one for someone who wants to simplify. For someone else, Sabbath Simplicity may look different. How it looks in your life depends on what your life is like now and how God is directing you. The key to Sabbath Simplicity is not just randomly eliminating activities or commitments. It's listening to God's direction and *then* doing what he tells you to do, whether that's cutting back, or trying some new things, or a combination of both. If you are focused on God, you'll see clearly what steps he wants you to take. Those will not likely be the same steps he directs someone else to take.

For many of us, Patti's starting point would be far simpler than we could imagine, compared to where we are now. By definition, *simplicity* is a relative term. We never arrive at Sabbath Simplicity—we take steps toward it. We increasingly focus on Christ and slowly prune away distractions from that.

Breathing Exercise

Sit and breathe slowly for a few minutes; reflect on Patti's story. What desires does it stir in you? What resonates with you? Do you ever have a day where you can simply rest? Do you even want to have that? Listen for God's direction on this issue.

Remember the Sabbath

The Bible commands us to rest. This is, when you think about it, amazing. What a generous and kind God we have. We expect marching orders, or hoops to jump through. But God simply says, "Alright, this will be challenging, but here's what I want you to do: take a break." That should be a no-brainer, right? So it's downright incredible that we so flagrantly disobey him on this.

As I've said, simplicity is all about having a "single eye," which means living with our primary focus on Christ. Keeping Sabbath is a great practice to help us maintain our focus. In the Jewish tradition, the Sabbath is the focus of the week, with three days to prepare for Sabbath, then following it, three days to reflect. This creates a rhythm of life that puts our focus not on our stuff or our schedule but on the opportunity to meet with God.

Does that sound anything like the way you live your life? Sure, you might not go to the office on Sunday, but do you keep yourself running with errands and busyness? Does Sunday look any different from the rest of the week, or is it just like Saturday, except you add church to the schedule?

Even if I stay home on Sunday afternoon, I find I am tempted to live in the future, rather than in the moment. I clip coupons from the paper, plan my week, plan meals, and make shopping lists. Is this really restful? Does this really keep me in the moment?

Going to church on Sunday can even become just another thing on our list of places to go and things to do. To rest requires intention. We need to be completely present, not thinking about the past or the future. To slow down requires thought. Although taking a break seems like a good idea, for some of us it's been so long since we did so we aren't sure why it's a good idea. For many of us, staying busy keeps us feeling important (although, again, we might not consciously realize that's what motivates us), and it's hard to give that up.

The Bible lists the Ten Commandments in Exodus and Deuteronomy. The Sabbath command is interesting because it doesn't just give a directive but also the rationale behind it. It's the longest command, because God elaborates a lot on what it means and why. And in the two lists, two different reasons are given.

Let's look at both passages. First, the Exodus version: Exodus 20:8–11 says, "Remember the Sabbath day by keeping it holy. Six days you shall labor and do all your work, but the seventh day is a Sabbath to the LORD your God. On it you shall not do any work, neither you, nor your son or daughter, nor your manservant or maidservant, nor your animals, nor the alien within your gates. For in six days the LORD made the heavens and the earth, the sea, and all that is in them, but he rested on the seventh day. Therefore the LORD blessed the Sabbath day and made it holy."

The Bible's rationale for the Sabbath is simple: we, God's image-bearers, function best by following God's example, particularly in how we manage our time. Resting on Sundays reminds us of the miracle of creation and the gift God gave himself and his creatures. It reminds us of how to dance the dance of life.

Learning to Dance

It's clear that God's intention with the commandment to remember the Sabbath is not that we would wake up Sunday morning and say, "Oh, yeah, that's right, it's the Sabbath." Rather, we need to always be remembering, Monday through Saturday, the Sabbath we just celebrated and the one that is coming.

Remembering the Sabbath is about a rhythm of life, a steady ebb and flow of work and rest. And it's about making one day holy, different, set apart.

In the creation account of Genesis, we see God establishing this rhythm of Sabbath Simplicity. Each day, he creates something, then steps back to evaluate. He gives himself a thumbs-up at the end of each day but then waits until the next day to get on with it.

He could have created all of life—the universe, from the vast to the microscopic—with a snap of his celestial fingers. He didn't. Why? I have a couple of theories. The first is Dallas Willard's thought that God is the most joyful being in the universe. And I think creating the cosmos was fun for him. He was having a good time. Can you imagine when he made aardvarks or zebras? I think he probably laughed.

When he finally got to people, man and woman, he probably felt great joy. Since we are made in his image, we are capable of finding great joy and happiness in our work. Sometimes, when I write, I get a glimpse of that. Do you ever find that joy in your work, in your ministry, in your parenting? In those moments when God gives you the right word to say to your kids or the patience and strength to love them, and you are so grateful that you get to be a mom? A moment of creative or exciting work that says, wow, I get to do this?

And after creating the cosmos, did God feel ready to collapse with exhaustion at the end of the week? Did he sigh and say, "Thank me it's Friday; I am so ready for the weekend!" No. He looked at the world, and especially the people he'd made, and said, "This is very good."

Having some people around, he rested with them. He didn't rest in solitude. He rested together with Adam and Eve. Hung out, perhaps shared a fruit salad. It was the first Shabbat meal. Theologian Karl Barth points out that on the seventh day, God's love takes form as time shared. God didn't rush through creation because he enjoyed it.

Second, I think God took his time creating the world because he wanted to show us a way of life from the very beginning. As I stated before, we are created in the image of God, and he modeled for us a way of life that makes sense for how we are created. Here's how to dance the dance of life, he said: work, be creative, use your imagination, throw yourself into it, whether you are washing dishes, reading to your kids and running a household, or trading stocks, reading corporate reports, and running a business. As the

Bible says, "Whatever you do, work at it with all your heart, as working for the Lord" (Col. 3:23).

At the end of each day, stop. Take a rest, eat a good meal, get enough sleep, and refresh yourself. Take time to think about your day, to notice where God was in it and where you were blessed, and to say, "It's good." Then go back at it the next day.

And after six days, take a whole day off. And say, "It's really good." Spend a whole day just pausing, just reflecting on how really good it is, and then start the dance again, at a sustainable pace.

Breathing Exercise

Does your life have a rhythm? Does it flow or move in fits and starts? What would your days look like if you paused at the end of each one to thank God and say, "It was good"? What would it take to start releasing some of your Sunday commitments so that a full day could be highlighted as "good"? What specific things could you do on Sundays to let your "love take form as time shared"?

Sabbath Freedom

The Deuteronomy account of the Ten Commandments differs slightly from the Exodus account. The fourth commandment is the same, and the beginning of the commandment is very similar to its counterpart in Exodus: "Observe the Sabbath day by keeping it holy, as the LORD your God has commanded you. Six days you shall labor and do all your work, but the seventh day is a Sabbath to the LORD your God. On it you shall not do any work, neither you, nor your son or daughter, nor your manservant or maidservant, nor your ox, your donkey or any of your animals, nor the alien within your gates, so that your manservant and maidservant may rest, as you do" (Deut. 5:12–14).

So far, an echo of the Sabbath command in Exodus. But in the next verse, God spells out a different reason for Sabbath-keeping. While it doesn't negate the first reason, it gives us more to ponder about this amazing command. "Remember that you were slaves in Egypt and that the LORD your God brought you out of there with a mighty hand and an outstretched arm. Therefore the LORD your God has commanded you to observe the Sabbath day" (Deut. 5:15).

God is reminding his people: You have choices. You are free. You are not slaves anymore; in fact, you might even have servants. Give yourself, and them, a day to rest. Remember and celebrate the fact that you have been set free.

Sabbath is about freedom.

Some people in Jesus's day and our day (and in the days in between) have turned Sabbath-keeping into bondage rather than freedom. We miss the gift if we get too legalistic, but we also miss it if we ignore Sabbath-keeping altogether.

The Bible says Jesus and his disciples worked hard but took time to rest as well. For Jesus, it wasn't just a day. Even on days other than the Sabbath, he would urge his disciples to come away and get some rest.

"The apostles gathered around Jesus and reported to him all they had done and taught," Mark reports in Mark 6. He continues: "Then, because so many people were coming and going that they did not even have a chance to eat, he said to them, 'Come with me by yourselves to a quiet place and get some rest.' So they went away by themselves in a boat to a solitary place" (vv. 30–32).

Can you relate? Do you ever long to simply sit down for a whole meal without interruptions, spills, or having to jump up and get something?

It's been said that the fourth commandment is the only one Christians like to brag about breaking. Why? I think, whether we are ministers or mothers, clerks or CEOs, we believe that if we are busy, we must be important.

To honor the Sabbath does not mean to run at mach speed for six days, then collapse in a trembling pile of adrenaline-wasted uselessness on Sunday—only to get up and run the rat race again the next day.

We have the freedom to make choices and live in a way that allows us to connect with God deeply on the Sabbath, and in fact, during the rhythm of our week.

Jesus was part of a culture that was Sabbath focused. The Sabbath was not just a day of rest but also a picture of Israel's covenant relationship with God and a reminder of the fact that God had redeemed his people from slavery.

In her book *Receiving the Day*, Dorothy Bass points out: "Slaves cannot skip a day of work, but free people can. Not all free people choose to do so, however; some of us remain glued to our computers and washing machines every day of the week. To keep Sabbath is to exercise one's freedom, to declare oneself to be neither a tool to be employed—an employee—nor a beast to be burdened. To keep Sabbath is also to remember one's freedom and to recall the One from whom that freedom came, and the One from whom it still comes."[2]

The Sabbath is a day, but keeping the Sabbath involves more than just one day.

Breathing Exercise

When you think about the Sabbath, how do you feel? What were Sundays like for you as a child? What appeals to you about a day of rest?

What objections or uncertainty arises as you consider the possibility of Sabbath-keeping? Reread the quote from Dorothy Bass above. What steps toward freedom would you like to take?

Hidden Gifts

In Jesus's time, the day before the Sabbath was called "Preparation Day." What we call Friday was the day to get things in order before the Sabbath. At sundown, all work had to cease. It just so happened that Jesus died on Preparation Day.

After Jesus died, a wealthy man named Joseph of Arimathea asked for and received Jesus's body. He quickly wrapped it in a cloth and put it in a tomb that he owned. He didn't have time to properly prepare the body for burial because it was late in the day.

Luke writes, "It was Preparation Day, and the Sabbath was about to begin. The women who had come with Jesus from Galilee followed Joseph and saw the tomb and how his body was laid in it. Then they went home and prepared spices and perfumes. But they rested on the Sabbath in obedience to the commandment" (Luke 23:54–56).

When someone in that culture died, it was customary to anoint the body with spices and perfumes. The women went home and, before sunset, quickly prepared those things. But they did not go to the tomb on the Sabbath. They waited.

What would have happened if they had blown off the Sabbath? I sometimes consciously disregard my Sabbath practice, citing some sort of cheap grace theory: "God will understand." Certainly, these women could have done that. They could have thought, "I know I'm supposed to rest, but Jesus's body is sitting there in a tomb, not properly anointed. Certainly God would understand; he would make an exception."

But they didn't do that. What if they had gone to the tomb on Saturday? Would they have missed the resurrection? Would they have been there too early?

What hidden gift did Mary Magdalene and the other women receive for their faithfulness in Sabbath-keeping?

"On the first day of the week, very early in the morning, the women took the spices they had prepared and went to the tomb. They found the stone rolled away from the tomb, but when they entered, they did not find the body of the Lord Jesus. While they were wondering about this, suddenly two men in clothes that gleamed like lightning stood beside them. In their fright the women bowed down with their faces to the ground, but the men said to them, 'Why do you look for the living among the dead? He is not here; he has risen!'" (Luke 24:1–6).

At first, the women might have regretted their Sabbath-keeping decision—while they rested, it appeared that someone had stolen Jesus's body from the tomb. As if that weren't bad enough, scary shiny people now appeared before them. But soon their fear and regret would turn to joy. Jesus has risen! Their Sabbath-keeping created space that brought them into an encounter with the living Christ.

Breathing Exercise

Read Luke 23:50–24:12. Read slowly. Imagine yourself to be one of the women in the story. How do you feel as you rest on the Sabbath? What are you thinking about? What fear or anxiety is at work in your heart? What do you experience (hear, see, feel) when you get to the tomb? Live in the story; reflect on it. What is God saying to you about Sabbath-keeping through this story?

Moms at Work

In my early career days, I loved my job and often spent fifty to sixty hours at it each week. Working that much, I looked forward to weekends. It was a time to hang out with friends, sleep in on Saturday, go to church on Sunday (okay, not every Sunday), or just relax. When I got married, my husband and I would often have friends over, go out, and enjoy the weekend away from our busy jobs.

Then I had kids. Suddenly, I did not get a day off; Saturday was just as busy as Monday. Diapers didn't take a day off. Toys got scattered all over every day of the week. If someone spit up, someone else had to clean it up, and that someone was typically me, no matter what day of the week it was. Even going to church, which I did a lot more regularly once I got married, took considerably more effort with a baby or two in tow.

But at least my husband was home on the weekends. We could go to church, perhaps get Chinese carryout. He'd take a turn walking the floor with the baby when she fussed, change a few diapers to give me a break. This was great. Then he changed jobs. His new career often kept him working longer hours. In order to provide for our family, he had to work evenings and most weekends.

I understood that, and I was grateful for the sacrifices he was making on our behalf. But I still found myself longing for a more life-giving rhythm of life. I felt as if I wasn't really accomplishing anything, but I still wanted a break. I wanted a weekend, not for socializing or going out, but for resting. I wanted a rhythm to my life rather than chaos. But the days blurred, one into another, and I sometimes had to look at the front of the newspaper to figure out what day it was.

I had grown up in a home where we had many comforting rhythms and routines: a family dinner every night at 6:30, church every Sunday. My mom even did laundry the same days every week: clothes on Monday, sheets and towels on Thursdays. She says she did this so she would not put off doing it. Having a specific day for certain chores helped keep them from slipping through the cracks.

At our home, traditions and routines were important, although there was flexibility and freedom. When I was younger, Sundays were quiet, relaxing days: church in the morning, sometimes brunch out. In the afternoons, we'd build a fire in the fireplace, go for a walk or a run, and maybe watch *Wide World of Sports* on TV. In other words, we'd spend the day just hanging with the family. I remember spending a lot of time reading the Sunday paper or a good book. In the summer, we'd spend some weekends camping or boating. But as my brother and I grew older, Sunday became a day, at least during certain seasons, for sports competition. So my dad would take my brother to his motorcycle race, while my mom took me to my sports events or practices.

I'd read the Bible, and I knew what Sabbath meant, sort of. I'd enjoyed the Sabbath (even though we didn't really call it that) as a child. But when motherhood took my casual weekends away, I became hungry for real rest. I didn't like being "on" every day of the week, and "on call" in a 24-7 kind of way.

At first, I asked my husband if he'd be willing to stay at home with the kids one night a week so I could have coffee with girlfriends. For a while, I did this, but I wanted something more. A couple of hours at Starbucks on a Tuesday evening was not enough, and it wasn't teaching my family about resting.

What if, despite the fact that I had to care for my kids, I could structure our week in such a way that we could have a day of relaxing and being together—to focus on God and his love for us, our love for each other? What if we said no just one day a week to the hectic craziness?

Over the years, I have slowly moved toward a life-giving style of Sabbath-keeping. No room for legalism or rules here. I'm still working out exactly what it looks like, and it seems to shift with seasons, both of the year and of life. What worked when my kids were three and five might not work now that they are seven and nine. We make accommodations for some things, like soccer games, but not for other things, like shopping. That's true of any spiritual discipline. What worked before I had kids doesn't fit now in the same way it did then. I don't always get it right, but I'm realizing that getting at least some of it right is a gift to my family and to myself.

Over the years, we have tried different ways of keeping the Sabbath, with varying degrees of success. Because my husband sells real estate, it's difficult for him to not work on Sunday, a prime selling day. Despite this, we've moved toward trusting God enough to take a day off. Sometimes we have made Wednesday our day of rest.

We're not always consistent. Last Sunday, for example, my husband wanted to get some work done, and he asked me to help. As much as I wanted a day of rest, I thought it over and decided that "resting" would mean refusing to help him in this particular instance, and that would not be the most loving choice. So I helped him with the tasks. We're obviously still figuring this stuff out.

The next weekend was Mother's Day. The only gift I asked for was that we have a day where none of us, especially my husband, worked. This was a difficult gift for him to give. ("Are you sure you don't just want some flowers?" he kept asking.) But he managed to actually rest that day and enjoyed it, which delighted me. The kids loved it too.

There are two sides to Sabbath: the deeper, more contemplative part that we label "spiritual" and the more practical side of slowing down, which is the discipline of Sabbath. We often want to skip the discipline part and move right on to the deep, meaningful part. The trouble is, the only way to get to the peace and joy and deeply spiritual part is by walking down the path of practicality. And all of it, the mundane, daily discipline and the "deep," is spiritual.

Breathing Exercise

What one specific step toward Sabbath Simplicity do you want to take as a result of what you have read in this chapter?

8

sheltered

How does Sabbath provide sanctuary?

My friend Naomi grew up in a Jewish home where faith traditions were very important. Central to the rhythm of their life was the Sabbath practice, which brought the family together every Friday evening.

"When I was growing up, Shabbat was about a family dinner on Friday night," she recalls. "My mom would light the Shabbat candles and say the prayer. My dad would pray over the wine and the bread. Today, there are shorter versions of Shabbat prayers, but my dad would do the whole thing, in Hebrew. The long version!

"In hindsight, it was grounding us in tradition. We had four kids in our family, and it forced us to be still. We did it all through high school. Even though at the time it felt like an imposition to my time with friends, I now remember this ritual and family time with such sweetness. They are warm memories."

When she went off to college, Naomi drifted away from the traditions of her Jewish faith. "I remembered it, but it was not sacred to me. I didn't feel compelled to observe the traditions and rituals," she says.

After college, she married John, who had been raised Catholic. Early in their marriage, they didn't practice any religion. She became pregnant but, sadly, suffered a miscarriage. It was a turning point in her faith journey.

"When I miscarried, my first thought was, 'I have to find a temple, I need sanctuary. I need grounding.' So I joined a temple, and John came with me. The people there embraced us as an interfaith couple."

Naomi was a spiritual seeker looking for rest for her soul.

At her new temple, Naomi instantly felt at home. Eventually, drawn by the acceptance of the community and the meaning he found in the Jewish faith, her husband converted. They had two boys, whom Naomi is raising in the Jewish faith. The rituals and rhythms of her faith create a simplicity in their lives—a comforting and meaningful predictability. Naomi continues on her spiritual journey, saying she has "very strong faith," in Jewish tradition, beliefs, and ancestry: God . . . the universe . . . mankind . . . all blended together. She knows that certain Jewish traditions bring her comfort and provide a restful place to pause in her life's journey.

"Shabbat to me is about family conversation. The dinner, the candles, the challah (special braided bread)," she says. "Then going to services after dinner. The services are held on Friday night about eight o'clock. We've taken the boys ever since they were babies. We'd sit in the third row, and the boys would fall asleep in our arms at service. It's a beautiful Shabbat memory."

Many people think of Saturday as the Jewish Sabbath, but because Sabbath begins at sundown on Friday, that Friday evening meal is an important element of the Shabbat practice and experience—the beginning of Shabbat. "Saturday is kind of a lazy day for our family, although many people choose to attend morning services and study groups as part of their practice. On Saturday evening, there is a sundown service, where you say good-bye to Shabbat and welcome the new week. This is a stunningly simple and beautiful practice, sweet and invigorating."

A traditional Shabbat dinner begins with the mother of the family praying as she lights candles to welcome the Sabbath. It also includes prayers over the wine, special bread, and other rituals. And on Saturday evening, the service (called Havdalah) also includes a spice box that is held while a special prayer is recited and the box is shaken to bring forth the beautiful aroma of the spices. "You smell it, and it awakens your senses," Naomi says. At each service, whether Shabbat or Havdalah, the candles, prayers, foods, sounds, and scents are the same each week. The meal engages all the senses as it draws the family together.

"I am comforted by most of the rituals even if I don't know all of the meaning behind each step and Hebrew word," Naomi says.

Simple Faith Grows Strong

Rituals can become especially significant when the regular routine of life is interrupted. And Naomi has dealt with some big interruptions along the way.

These began when her older son, then five years old, was diagnosed with cancer. The family found themselves suddenly focused on dealing with a serious illness and wrestling with all the physical, spiritual, and emotional struggles associated with it.

The situation was tough on the young family. Her boys had always been close, and Naomi says her second born felt his brother's pain in a deep way and wrestled with his own fears and doubts. Her children's journey inspired Naomi to found and run a nonprofit organization to support families of children with cancer, which today is her full-time work. But at the time, she was just trying to hang on as she went through an ordeal that both tested and strengthened her faith.

"I remember one time when my son was in the hospital, I felt I needed to go to Shabbat services. I needed sanctuary and needed peace in my familiar community," she recalls. "We decided to go to a service at a temple near our hospital. Since my son couldn't go, he had sent with us a list of kids on the cancer floor to pray for while we were at Shabbat services.

"During the service, the rabbi was telling us to be thinking of people in need of healing: physical, emotional, spiritual. He asked us to say the names out loud of those we wanted to pray for. We had this handwritten list from my five-year-old. We read it out loud at the service. It was so moving, not just for us, but for others there. That service was like an anchor in an uncertain time."

Her son has been cancer-free for more than five years. But the family's struggles didn't end there. Naomi and John divorced this year, and they live apart but within a few miles of each other so that they can share custody of the boys. The split was amicable, but the change is difficult.

"Now we are in two houses, and the boys are with their father on Friday night," she says. "It breaks my heart. But I know they have a strong Jewish identity. They still go to Hebrew school. It's part of the fabric woven into our lives. And I try to find other ways to weave our faith into everyday acts together and in our conversations."

While Naomi is trusting that the boys will continue on their spiritual journey, she has found that being single again has made "rest for her soul" somewhat elusive.

"It was an adjustment to be alone on Friday nights," Naomi says. "It hurt. But now I usually celebrate Shabbat with some friends. One friend, right now, is in a nursing home. Sometimes on Shabbat I go and visit her and sing prayers for her. It gives her family comfort to know someone is there, and they can go to services. Before this, I wouldn't equate doing something like that with Shabbat, but I think now it's especially appropriate."

The trials Naomi has endured have taught her a lot about the importance of her faith. She doesn't have it all figured out, but as she continues on her spiritual journey, she knows she needs to pause and catch her breath sometimes.

"My life is so hectic," she said. "I have to sometimes slow down and create some space. When I tuck the boys in at night, I rub their backs, and I look at them. Really look into their eyes, and thank God, remembering. I take my time and appreciate that they are alive and healthy. I look at them lying there in peace. And when I wake them up in the mornings, I look at them again, and we greet the day together. Sometimes we say the Shema together. It's a holy prayer: 'Hear, O Israel: The Lord our God, the Lord is one.'"

Naomi adds that Jews like to point out that even the name of their prayer, Shema, is a word made of these peaceful breathing sounds. Shhhh. Ummmm. Ahhhh. Say it slowly and it relaxes you. It's a reminder that God is closer than the air we breathe.

Breathing Exercise

Sit and take a few deep breaths. Try praying the Shema: "Hear, O Israel: The Lord our God, the Lord is one." Shhhh. Ummmm. Ahhhh. Be still. Take some time to reflect on Naomi's story. How do you respond? What do you want to add to your practice of Sabbath Simplicity as a result of hearing her story? Tonight when you tuck your children in, take some time to look into their eyes and thank God that they are alive.

Shaping the Day

As you can see from the stories of the women we've met so far in this book, Sabbath-keeping can vary widely in how it is practiced, depending on your circumstances and your background, as well as your personality. The best way to start living Sabbath Simplicity is to embrace the fact that because you are imperfect, your spiritual practices are going to be imperfect, but God loves you anyway.

If you actually do begin to practice Sabbath-keeping, you'll have to make some choices. From a practical standpoint, you have to decide what your Sabbath will look like. What activities would you like to refrain from? Also, just as important, what do you want to include? What is restful?

Perhaps you will decide that you will, as Naomi does, look into the eyes of the people you love and really appreciate that they are alive and with you.

Perhaps you're more pragmatic and understand it might be good to simply refrain from shopping on Sundays. This makes sense to me. First, our shopping requires others to work. Second, "fasting" from shopping is a radical act in a country where we are often identified not as persons but as "consumers." I do not want my primary identity to be "consumer." Some people, especially women, believe

"I shop, therefore, I am." But something in me wants to stand up and say, "That's not me. I am, whether I shop or not!" To keep out of the mall on Sundays is to say, "I am more than just the thing I consume or purchase."

In addition to resting from shopping, I take a rest from housework. I don't do laundry or cleaning on Sundays. But freedom has a price. I try to keep the place picked up throughout the week. (Big emphasis on "try." Ask my friends about how I interpret "keeping the place picked up" and they will laugh and tell you that at least I have good intentions.) I do laundry during the week. I clean thoroughly on Friday and Saturday (okay, some weeks more thoroughly than others). It's motivating to know that I'm cleaning the house not so my family can mess it up again (a rather defeatist attitude) but so that we can rest together in an orderly environment.

During the week, I cook things ahead so I won't have to spend Sunday in the kitchen. We sometimes have a Crock-Pot meal that I do most of the prep work for on Saturday.

I know a woman who told her kids that they could not do homework on Sundays. They were delighted, even though it meant they had to get the work done Friday or Saturday. Again, freedom has a price, but her kids were glad to pay it because it made Sundays so much more enjoyable.

These simple ideas illustrate how the Sabbath spills over into the days prior to it. The Sabbath is not a one-day event; it's a cycle, a rhythm for life. But housework and cooking are not the only preparations necessary. To keep the Sabbath, I need not only to rest but also to redirect my attention to God. It's the purpose for resting. Not just to slow for the sake of slowing but to open space for God in my life—to focus on him rather than on myself and my needs.

Breathing Exercise

If you were to take a Sabbath from chores like cooking and cleaning, how would you have to order your week? What day would you have to grocery shop? What would you have to do to prepare? Write the chores, such as cleaning and shopping, on your calendar. Make it a goal this week to eliminate just a few of the things that keep your Sundays too busy. What steps can you take this month to gradually eliminate hurry from your Sabbath day?

Imperfect Sabbath-keeping

Again, Sabbath Simplicity is easier if you accept from the get-go that you will never get it perfect. In fact, Sabbath Simplicity is about letting go of your perfectionism.

This happened to me on one imperfect Sabbath. That Sunday, it snowed. We went to church, bundling the kids into boots, mittens, and warm jackets. When we got home, Scot went to work. On a perfect Sabbath, there would be no slush on my floor and my husband would be home with us, perhaps leading us in a family devotional time. Pop! That was the bubble bursting on the sharp edge of reality. But does that mean I should just give up on Sabbath? Of course not. On many other Sabbaths, Scot is home, and we read the Bible with the kids. But those weeks, we don't get all the other things on our "perfect Sabbath" list checked off. And that is okay!

This particular snowy day, the kids and I made it a day of being at home, doing quiet, simple, ordinary things. We had space to do them because we weren't trying to run around and do errands or accomplish anything. The kids played out in the snow; we had soup and sandwiches for lunch; we cuddled on the couch.

In our backyard are several large trees, home to a family of fat and sassy squirrels. We put bread out on the stump for the squirrels, and my daughter decided she wanted to write a note to the squirrels. So her crayon drawing sat there, behind the crusts.

We sat near the window and waited for the squirrels to come down the tree to discover their meal. Melanie sat watching, then was suddenly filled with regret and doubt about the note to the squirrels. It was as if she suddenly realized, "What if squirrels can't read?"

For me, it was a chance to live in the present moment, to be aware of where she's at and where she's going. She's in a time of transition, from little girl to bigger girl. The little girl wants to believe the squirrels can not only read but are also able to deeply appreciate the sentiments in her note. The little girl names the squirrels, her favorite being the fattest one, Tubby. The bigger girl within her scoffs at that. She's conflicted. I told her I love everything about her, especially her imagination and the way she loves animals, and the way that she is figuring out who she is.

We sat in a chair, Melanie on my lap, and simply watched a squirrel nibble a bread crust for about fifteen minutes (they were pretty stale crusts!). We didn't say a whole lot following the discussion of whether squirrels could read. (I told her I didn't know, but that they understood clearly the message of caring and love in the gift of bread crusts.) I chose not to pull away from her until she was ready and stood up without my asking.

Later, Aaron and I lay on the couch, and I rubbed his feet while he looked at a book. We did not turn on the TV, despite occasional requests from the kids. They said they were bored more than once. I responded with attention and love. Stories, not lectures. The no-TV was not a punishment but a chance to read together, to connect, to have quiet. We put on Christmas music for a while, and the kids danced and sang along. We built a fire in the fireplace. I read the newspaper. We rested. Late in the afternoon, the kids had some friends over, and they played in the basement. Dinner was leftovers, but we ate together as a family, talking about what we had learned in church and what we saw the squirrels doing. The kids went to bed early. I told Scot about the squirrels and the tender moments with Melanie, and we wondered together at the gift of our children.

Sabbath is not about rule-keeping; it's about creating space. In addition to preparing my home, I want to prepare my heart.

"Sabbath is more than the absence of work; it is not just a day off, when we catch up on television or errands. It is the presence of something that arises when we consecrate a period of time to listen to what is most deeply beautiful, nourishing, or true. It is a time consecrated with our attention, our mindfulness, honoring those quiet forces of grace or spirit that sustain and heal us," writes Wayne Muller.[1]

Breathing Exercise

How do you think slowing your pace for just one day would affect the pace of the rest of your week? Would it teach you to go slower or would it make the rest of your week more hectic? Set aside next Sunday (or at least the one after that) to try it and see.

A Real Rest

Maybe you seek rest, but you are not sure how to get there. Some of us find we are able to occasionally enjoy rest and recreation, but we see them as completely compartmentalized from our spiritual lives. We've got our "spiritual" stuff in one box, our "work" in another, and our "recreation" (often extremely competitive or dangerously escapist) in a third. They never connect. But that doesn't sound like living freely and lightly.

For some of us, depending on how legalistic our background is, Sabbath might seem like a restrictive or punitive deal. Or it may be something we feel we want but don't have the foggiest notion how to access.

Finding Sabbath rest, regularly practicing the Sabbath, will form our spirit into the image of Christ. When we find rest in Sabbath, that quietness can spill over into our lives, including our prayer life and our communion with God.

"One translation of the biblical phrase 'to pray' is 'to come to rest.' When Jesus prayed he was at rest, nourished by the healing spirit that saturates those still, quiet places," Wayne Muller writes. "In the Jesus tradition, prayer can be a practice of simply being in the presence of God, allowing the mind to rest in the heart. This can help us begin to understand one aspect of Sabbath time: a period of repose, when the mind settles gently in the heart."[2]

In my own journey, I have sought Sabbath. I am finding it in the embracing of a paradox: Sabbath is about freedom but also about surrender. It's trusting God to act, but it's also about making choices and acting on them. It's trusting God enough to follow his lead and to use my freedom to make choices that will ultimately give me rest.

As a Christian writer and speaker, I have a lot of great theories about Sabbath-keeping. As a soccer mom and wife of a man who often has to work weekends, those theories get tested regularly.

I do know this: my ability to live as Jesus would in my place and my desire to act like him, talk to him, include him in my life, ebbs and flows. Maybe that ebb and flow has something to do with my focus, my ability to listen. As I try to understand why there are times when I wrestle with sin and other times when it seems perfectly natural to consult God on every decision and obey him, it has come down to this: what is the pace of my life?

Sabbath-keeping is about choices: to engage in spiritual disciplines or practices that will allow your desire for Sabbath rest to become a reality. Making the choice not to hurry. Sabbath-keeping cannot be an add-on to a hectic, scattered life. By definition, it is a part of a mindful, sanely paced, God-focused life.

Sabbath Simplicity, of which Sabbath-keeping is a crucial part, keeps me on the track of spiritual growth. When I get too busy, even with ministry or family, I am more easily tempted to sins of pride. I don't listen to others or to God very well when I'm rushed. So why would I choose this?

Keeping Sabbath Together

Sabbath-keeping is something we can and should do in community. We gather to worship. Perhaps, like Naomi, we give the gift of our presence to another person without expecting anything in return. While part of our practice is individual, such as spending time in prayer and private contemplation, the Sabbath is also meant to be shared with others.

If you typically don't eat meals together as a family, a great place to begin your Sabbath journey is by setting aside one weekend night to have dinner together and talk about where you have seen God in your lives.

You may want to do something recreational together as a family: anything from going for a walk or a bike ride to going skiing; whatever it is you enjoy.

My husband and I like to spend our summer Sundays sailing. It's a chance for us to have fun together and "unplug" from obligations, cell phones, work. We laugh and have fun; we don't talk about bills or schedules or anything stressful. We reconnect as a couple, not by having deep discussions about our marriage but by simply having a good time.

Some families pick a Scripture passage that they will discuss as part of their family Sabbath practice. They prepare for the Sabbath by meditating on that Scripture during the week, then they discuss it around the dinner table on Sunday.

You don't have to start with a whole day. Start with an hour, where you eat slowly together and move on from there.

What should you do or not do on the Sabbath? I can't tell you. I am learning that the Sabbath is not about rules. The Pharisees made up all kinds of rules about Sabbath-keeping and squeezed the joy right out of it.

The Sabbath is about listening to God. It's a mind-set of trust and a time for rest and reflection. Maybe you could try really looking at, and being deeply grateful for, your family members the way Naomi does. Perhaps you could choose not to shop one day per week. What could you do that is truly restful?

Make Sabbath the focus of your week. Live your entire week in such a way that you can truly enjoy your day; use it to connect with God and the people you love and who love you.

As you continue seeking Sabbath, know that ultimately, you are seeking God; rest in this promise found in Jeremiah 29:12–14: "'Then you will call upon me and come and pray to me, and I will listen to you. You will seek me and find me when you seek me with all your heart. I will be found by you,' declares the LORD."

Breathing Exercise

What refreshes and rejuvenates you? What brings you joy? How could you dedicate a day (or even half a day to start) to doing those things? What would you like to say no to doing, even for just one day?

Take a look at your schedule during the week. Remember, you can't live in Sabbath Simplicity without preparing ahead of time.

What could you eliminate or delegate? What will you need to get done on the other days in order to avoid doing things like laundry or shopping on Sundays? How might you invite your family into a time of Sabbath refreshment or recreation?

part five

the reassurance

For my yoke is easy,
and my burden is light

9

slow

What keeps me moving too fast?

Grace remembers the afternoon clearly. She had just come home from her four-year-old son's basketball class and was getting ready to go out again: packing a diaper bag for her one-year-old and collecting snacks, crayons, and juice boxes to keep her two young boys occupied while they sat through her music rehearsal at church. She searched for her sheet music and then reviewed her songs to be sure she was prepared for the rehearsal. Grabbing her purse, she directed her boys to hurry up and get ready to go.

"Knowing how long it usually took us just to get out the door, I had started an hour before we actually had to leave, making sandwiches and getting their shoes and jackets on, all the way telling them to hurry up," she remembers. "I felt myself getting caught in the onslaught of major necessary details and sort of knowing—okay, this is the part where I get frantic and anxious. But it had become routine, as had my tendency to get rather short with the boys, to speak a bit abruptly to them."

In the midst of the hurricane that was his mother, little four-year-old Matthew suddenly stood in the middle of the mudroom with his arms out, palms facing forward, as if to steady himself or perhaps to motion her to stop. He looked up at her. "Mom," he said forcefully, "you are moving too fast."

Grace was so stunned that she sat down on a bench and stared at her son. He looked at her, perhaps uncertain of what to say next. "It's not good when you run me," he added.

"I started crying," she says. "And then of course he came up and patted my arm and said, 'It's okay, Mom.' He wanted to comfort me. But what struck me was that a four-year-old was able to name with such clarity the thing I could not."

Grace never made it to rehearsal that day. She called and said she couldn't make it. Unfortunately, ruthlessly eliminating hurry is never that simple.

Grace was more than just a voice in the choir. In fact, her church usually didn't have a traditional choir, but rather a small group of vocalists leading worship at each service. One missing person would be conspicuous. Because of that format and the group members' dedication, missing rehearsals was something that simply wasn't done. So it came as a surprise to the other vocalists that although Grace wasn't sick and hadn't lost her voice, she simply wasn't coming to practice.

Because of what Matthew said, Grace realized that the choices she had made about time commitments and the pace of her life were hindering her growth. She was saying yes when she ought to say no. She really wanted to change the way she was living her life, but she wasn't sure how. After all, like Grace herself, her friends on the music team seemed to thrive on the breakneck pace of their ministry.

She had given up a fast-paced corporate job to start a family, to be an at-home mom. The problem was, she was rarely at home, and she was still rather fast paced. She kept herself moving quickly, pretty much by choice. Her life as a mother of two toddlers was already requiring lots of time, but on top of that, she was volunteering a lot of her time at church. The church was growing rapidly, and everyone who volunteered or served on the staff worked hard, buoyed by the excitement of the church's impact on the community.

She was a talented vocalist often asked to sing solos. That meant serving not only at the multiple weekend services but also attending a long Tuesday evening rehearsal, typically with her two young boys in tow. Sometimes she would sing at a midweek service as well or for several days in a row when the church hosted pastors' conferences. She also traveled to conferences overseas and around the country as part of her ministry team.

Grace was involved in other ways at church, so the kids were sometimes in the church nursery, sometimes with her in meetings or rehearsals, sometimes at home with her husband or a sitter. She was often at church more nights during the week than she was at home.

"I had transferred the same frenetic style I had in the corporate world into my parenting and even my serving at church," she says.

She knew she was moving too fast; she wasn't sure why. But she knew God was speaking to her through her four-year-old. In a decision that changed her life, she chose to listen. That was just the beginning of a long process of looking at the truth about herself and how she had chosen to live her life.

"That day, the dam broke," she says. "It [the confrontation with Matthew] pushed me into a time of self-examination. Why was I continuing to live in this unhealthy pattern? It was the start of finding out what a false self I'd been projecting. I was finally willing to admit that there were limitations to *me*."

The ministry she served in was a hard environment in which to attempt change. "No one was pioneering or modeling for me what a healthy way to set priorities was," she says. "I look back and realize that part of this false self I was presenting to people was because I really hoped someone would say, 'Wow, you have this amazing endless capacity—you win the award.'"

On the advice of a friend from church, Grace spent some time talking with a wise Christian counselor who helped her know what questions to ask herself as she spent more time in quiet and self-examination.

"On my second visit with her, my counselor very calmly said, 'Have you considered taking a sabbatical?' And my gut reaction was, 'Can I do that? Is that allowed?'" Grace recalls. "She looked at me and very gently said, 'Oh, *they* don't let you. You have to choose it.' I realized that I had turned control of my life over to other people."

Grace found it hard to actually make the decision to take a break. Not until several months after the interaction with her son in the mudroom did she finally decide to take time off from serving at church. For eight months, she simply stopped all of her volunteering. Stopping created a tension that she had to wrestle with: Did she still have value if she wasn't being "productive"? Was it enough to simply focus for a season on nurturing her relationships with her children and husband? With God?

"Initially, it felt scary," she says. "But gradually, the benefits became apparent. It was so wonderful to 'waste' time with my kids. But it was hard to keep other things from taking the place of what had made me busy before."

The Easy Yoke

What did Grace do during that time off? Well, of course, she was able to give much more attention to her family and managing her home. But knowing how hurried and frantic she'd been, Grace decided she also needed to spend some time just being quiet. That summer she hired a neighborhood high school girl to watch the boys for a few hours each Thursday. She did not use the time to run errands, shop, or even get together with a friend. Instead, she went to a local nature preserve, taking her journal and art supplies. She sketched, she read, she painted, she simply sat and noticed the beauty of the marsh, the woods, the birds. In her journal on the first day she did this, she wrote that she had reached a turning point. "I'm here to spend two hours being still and being with my Lord . . . and asking him to feed my hungry, starved soul."

She embraced solitude and silence in a way she never had. She knew she was onto something, because she felt a deep peace and joy in her heart.

"People noticed the change," she admits, adding that, because she was now saying no, some people were not too enthused about the new Grace. "I knew I needed time for myself to reacquaint myself with God and to develop intimacy with him. It had been such a long time since I had listened. I was soul-starved."

Thankfully, her husband, Tim, applauded her decision, as did her counselor and a trusted friend. They encouraged her to continue to stay in the way of life that God was obviously calling her to.

The process didn't happen overnight. Grace felt guilt and frustration over how she had spent her first four years of being a mom. God graciously healed that sadness over time, often by helping Grace to simply laugh and not take herself quite so seriously.

On a Sunday afternoon not long after the "mudroom incident" but before her sabbatical, Grace sat to relax and catch her breath in a chair on the lawn after singing at church that morning. "I think this was the day I really became a mom," she says. "I was outside, and the boys were out with me, and they were gravitating toward this big mud puddle near the driveway. I could see them eyeing it, and I was getting annoyed. They were going to get dirty, and I didn't like that idea. My knee-jerk reaction was to jump up and stop the nonsense, to keep them out of the mud. But it was like something pushed me back into my chair. I thought, *Why not?* They stomped into that puddle and started to smear mud on each other. At first, they looked over to see what I would do. When I didn't stop them, they got bold. Slowly, they started just smearing mud on their legs, their arms, each other. Their arms looked like they had black gloves up to the elbow. I just sat there and watched them and laughed. I realized I had turned a corner—I didn't have to control them so much. They were so happy. I realized it was okay for my kids to be kids."

Today, more than twelve years later, Grace lives her life much differently than she did before. "I think my four-year-old saved my life," she says simply.

"We Are Not in a Hurry"

Grace became dedicated to practicing solitude, something she did not "have time for" before. The practice of "slowing" created space for other practices that deepened her faith and her relationship with God. Her starved soul was being fed by the quiet, by the chance to talk to God in a leisurely way. She was experiencing the easy yoke in a way she never had before. Her afternoons off grew longer and more frequent. Once the boys became school age, she would make sure that she spent part of the time they were gone just being still and listening to God by praying, reflecting on Scripture, or working quietly in her garden.

"I became dangerously contemplative," she laughs. "For a while, the boys would say to Tim, 'Please, don't let Mom pray at dinner,' because I'd thank God for every tree in the yard, for the birds, for all the flowers, for each thing that happened that day. They were afraid the food would get cold before I'd finish."

She still had a busy life. Eventually, she went back to serving at church but carefully limited the amount of time she spent there. The boys went to a private school, so she had to drive them there. They were both athletic, playing soccer and baseball. Her life was full, but she made sure to carve out time to learn and to be quiet. She would sometimes leave the boys with her husband and go away for a weekend of spiritual retreat, either by herself or with a close friend or two.

These practices became a way of life that transformed her. Jesus's yoke, she was discovering, was not about serving in a workaholic fashion. It was about simply being with him and letting that change her heart. It was taking on his way of life, his contemplative, prayerful, loving way of life. It meant practicing the things he modeled for us, like solitude, prayer, and silence. These practices began to transform her heart, and thus, slowly, her new way of life began to change the way she interacted with family, friends, and even strangers.

Grace told me recently of taking her boys to a travel baseball game and stopping at a fast-food restaurant. The circumstances (fast food, travel baseball) could make someone feel hurried. The place was busy and got busier when the boys' team descended on the place for breakfast. The workers behind the counter were frantically filling orders. Grace stepped up to the counter with her now teenage boys and paused. Here's where she chose to think differently, to be fully present. To act as Jesus would if he had breakfast with the team at McDonald's.

The man behind the counter looked at her.

"Good morning, sir," Grace said. "How are you?"

The man looked startled, then answered, "Well, we're really busy."

"Sir, I need to tell you something," Grace said, her voice calm, her eyes looking kindly into his. "We are not in a hurry." She paused again, then smiled warmly at the man. "All these other people, they may be in a hurry, but we are not."

Matthew, who is now taller than his mother, shrugged at the man and rolled his eyes as if to say, "Don't blame me for this."

Grace said the worker looked at her in shock for a minute, then smiled and took their order. He did not hurry them along. Rather, he supersized their orange juices without their asking and offered extra hash browns. He thanked them for dining at the Golden Arches and really meant it.

So how did she get there? How did Grace move from being a woman who was told by a preschooler that she was moving too fast to a mom who, in the midst of chaos, could ruthlessly eliminate hurry and make an overworked minimum-wage earner feel loved and appreciated? By listening to Jesus's invitation to drop the heavy burden of impressing people and taking up his yoke, his way of life. A decade of contemplative practice has made her a more patient person.

"I had to retrain my heart," she says. "It was very hard, but I knew if I didn't make these changes, I would turn out how I did not want to be. God showed me that, but he never shamed me. Over the years I have developed such a sweetness of communion with him. Being with him in solitude, especially in nature, I am refueled and refilled. It never really worked to operate out of an empty tank. But countless things masquerade as the real deal. So many things call us to destruction or just distraction. They keep us from God."

Grace has grown so much, in part because she was willing to create space in her life, to exchange the burdens she carried for the light burden of loving others that Christ calls us to, not alone but in partnership with him.

Breathing Exercise

Take a blank sheet of paper or turn to a blank page in your journal. Draw a tree and label its branches with various obligations and commitments of your life. Make one large branch for each member of your family and for major areas that take up your time, such as ministry, housework, work outside the home, volunteering, and so forth. Draw smaller branches coming off each one to represent the things you do for each "branch" that take up your time and energy.

Once your drawing is complete, sit and look at it. What comes to mind? Is the tree lopsided? Journal about how this picture makes you feel. Pray about what God might want you to prune from your commitments. You can't prune off the branch that represents your two-year-old, but perhaps you could prune some of the smaller branches. Maybe you could talk to your spouse about taking on some of your child's care— such as giving him his bath or taking him to the park to play on Saturday mornings. Don't prune arbitrarily. Listen to God's voice. Don't prune too much at one time. Keep this drawing and come back to it every few weeks or so. Be open to further pruning.

A Hurried Heart

What would it take for you to slow down enough to live as Jesus would? Maybe you don't have a lot on your calendar; maybe you don't keep overly busy outside of the house, but you still feel overwhelmed. If you have very young children, it's likely that you don't write out a schedule, because that would only be depressing. Imagine it, with things such as:

5:00 a.m.   Nurse baby

5:30 a.m.   Put baby back to bed

5:35 a.m.   Baby cries, waking other child and husband

5:40 a.m.   Get up; sigh

5:45 a.m.   Balance baby on one hip while pouring cereal for toddler and attempting to converse with cranky husband

5:50 a.m.   Wipe up spilled milk while holding screaming baby . . .

Okay, it's starting to get a little depressing. A little while later in the day, you'd add:

10:00 a.m.   Play Chutes and Ladders with toddler while nursing baby, until eyes cannot focus anymore

11:00 a.m.   Is it lunchtime yet?

11:05 a.m.   Refuse to play one more game of Chutes and Ladders

11:10 a.m.   Agree to play Chutes and Ladders if it means not having to play Candyland or sing all fifteen verses of "The Wheels on the Bus"

11:15 a.m.   Yes, it definitely is lunchtime

11:45 a.m.   Park kids in front of television in order to clean up kitchen from utter disaster created by attempting to get two small people to eat lunch

Noon   Feel guilty for letting kids watch too much television

12:05 p.m.   Get over guilt by sitting down to watch *Barney* with them

12:45 p.m.   Nap time for kids

12:46 p.m.   Finally take shower . . .

A hurried heart doesn't always come from having a busy schedule. Sometimes it comes from feeling overwhelmed by the daily demands of just keeping your children alive and the house still standing. It is possible to simplify, to slow down. Begin with awareness.

No matter what stage of life you are in, if you feel hurried, you can slow down. And slowing down won't just make you less hurried; it will create space for God. Letting God into that space will begin to transform your soul.

Living in the Moment

Speed is relative. Before you can figure out how to slow down, you have to figure out how fast you are going. The earlier "Breathing Exercise" where you drew branches can help with that. But the externals of your schedule and your life are only part of what makes you hurried.

We live in a fast-paced world. But often it is our thinking that gets us into trouble. Our worry about how busy we are, rather than our actual busyness, stresses us out. That is because unhealthy thinking, especially worry, takes us away from the present moment.

Worry is based on fear. Think about a time you felt worried. Were you focused on the moment you were in? Most likely, you were worried about something in the future (a test or meeting or some perceived obstacle that you were anticipating trouble with) or else you were worried about the past (did your friend take what you said the wrong way; did you make a fool of yourself; why did you lose your temper or overeat or forget an appointment?).

Slowing down requires not only pruning your schedule but also changing your thinking. If you are always thinking about past mistakes or future concerns, you can't think about the present moment. You can't be fully present, so you will feel hurried.

Richard Carlson and Joseph Bailey explore this idea in greater depth in their book *Slowing Down to the Speed of Life*. They note that many people want to slow down, so they make dramatic, sometimes costly changes in their lifestyle. (You know, quit the high-powered career and move to a log cabin in the mountains or something along those lines.) But hurry, at its root, is not about lifestyle or where you live. It's about how you think and how you perceive the world. It's about whether you are able to be in the present moment or get stuck worrying about the past or the future.

"Lifestyle changes alone rarely make a real difference," Carlson and Bailey write. "You can rearrange the externals of your life in a radically different way, but you always take your thinking with you. If you are a hurried, rushed person in the city, you'll also be a hurried, rushed person in the country."[1]

This is good news. (No, *really*, it is!) That's because many people can't make huge lifestyle changes. You live where you do, and sometimes circumstances prevent you from making a radical move. If you are the parent of a baby and a toddler, that's who you are; you can't change this fact (although circumstances will change as the children grow). But if you are a hurried, rushed parent with a baby, you'll eventually be a hurried, rushed parent of a teenager. The trick is to change the way you think. That's where the good news comes in: it is possible to change the way you think.

Carlson and Bailey say the key to slowing down is to notice your thinking. You're always thinking, whether you are aware of it or not. The feeling of being overwhelmed or hurried often comes, they say, when your thinking spins out of control, so that you are no longer aware of your thinking. Training yourself to notice your thoughts and feelings will help you slow down, they write.

"When we spend too much time reliving the past, we are, by definition, not in the moment. Time spent regretting or feeling guilty, embarrassed, or resentful is going to keep you from experiencing the present. Of course there are things we regret, feel guilty about and wish others hadn't done, but spending time thinking about them will increase the chances of repeating the error and the pain associated with past errors."[2]

Taking the authors' concept to the next step, if we can notice our thinking, we can slow down enough to pray about it. We not only can say, "Wow, I'm feeling really cranky," but then we can take the next step and say, "God, I'm feeling frustrated and angry. Help me to slow down enough to figure out what I ought to do."

We're not denying our feelings, but we're going to let God hold them while we replace them with some positive, affirming thoughts.

The gift that comes from telling God about our feelings and thoughts is that he understands us. Once we have told him, we don't feel so compelled to spew our anger at the people around us. When we name our fear or frustration, we can decide to take our thoughts in another direction. God understands. If we embrace the fact that we are fully understood, yet still fully loved, we are empowered to change our thinking. With the help of the one who loves us so unconditionally, we can choose to take a deep breath and choose to change our thinking. He can transform us through our mind. As the apostle Paul says, "Do not conform any longer to the pattern of this world, but be transformed by the renewing of your mind" (Rom. 12:2):

Breathing Exercise

As you go through your day, pay attention. Notice when you feel flustered, hurried, overwhelmed. Stop for a second and name what's going on in your mind and heart. Say to yourself, "I'm feeling . . ." and fill in the blank. Don't try to change the way you feel, just notice it. Tell God about it, since he's right there, as close as your next deep breath.

Push the Pause Button

If you are not sure about your thoughts or feelings, you can become more aware of them by incorporating the practice of pausing into your life. Noticing your out-of-control thoughts is one way to pause. Taking a deep breath or saying a breath prayer is another.

If we had no punctuation or spaces in this book, everysentencewouldlooklikethisanditwouldbehardtoreadandevenhardertounderstand.

It is the space in between that gives words their meaning.

It is the spaces you put in your day that help you understand the meaning of all your work, all your striving. Pausing reminds you to be mindful, to be aware, to look for God in the midst of all the craziness.

Sometimes we just need to pause for a minute. Some of us do this already when we pause to pray, such as before meals. There is as much value in the pausing as there is in the praying. Some people pray when they get behind the wheel of a car, asking God for traveling mercies.

If we are about to confront someone, we often pause, gathering our thoughts and taking a deep breath before we say, "I need to talk to you about something." If we are about to make a key decision, we reflexively hit the brakes.

We pause for a moment (sometimes longer) and say, "Let me think about this." Pausing helps us gather our thoughts, forcing us to slow down in order to think more clearly, to become aware of how we are feeling.

Pausing is not the same as collapsing. Some people say, "I'll do all my pausing at the end of the day, after the kids are in bed." That's not hitting the brakes; that's running out of gas. Both get you stopped, but only one is intentional. And only one will help you feel more rested and peaceful.

Do you ever pause? As you move from one activity to the next, do you stop and just breathe for a minute? This discipline is hard for me, because I have trouble staying on one thing at a time. I'll be emptying the dishwasher and realize that the counters need to be wiped before I can set the dishes on them, so I'll start clearing the counters, then find something on them that needs to go to another room in the house, so I'll take it there, and then I'll see that the kids have spilled something in that room, so I'll clean it up, and then the dryer will buzz and I'll go to get the clothes out, then put in another load of laundry, then notice that nobody fed the dog, and then I go back in the kitchen and think I ought to put the dirty dishes from the sink into the dishwasher, and then sigh because the dishwasher is open and the clean plates have still not been put away. . . . I don't pause between activities because I never really finish one activity at a time. I have been working on this by saying out loud to myself: "Stay focused; stay focused. Finish the task."

It's easier to pause if you've actually finished something. Maybe you're like me; you need to work on finishing each task. Maybe you are already good at this, but you still don't stop to catch your breath.

During your day, pausing can take the form of simply sitting still for one minute, taking a break to talk to a friend or co-worker after completing a task at work, or taking a break from household chores to just snuggle with your kids. When you pause, be mindful of the rest you are giving your body. Don't be thinking about the next thing on your to-do list. Simply rest, even for a minute.

Building pauses into your day will help you to slow down. It will remind you to focus on Jesus, to simplify. Begin with very short pauses and work up to longer ones. Start with a couple of pauses, perhaps just before and after each meal, then, as you get better at this practice, pause more often. Just remembering to breathe is a good start. Taking a daylong pause once a week for a Sabbath is another way of pausing. If you think that would be impossible, start small. If you can pause for a few minutes, you can gradually learn to take longer times of rest.

If I want to create space for God in my life, I have to first create space. Space . . . pauses . . . give life meaning.

"The space we give words—whether those words are the text of Scripture or the texts of our daily lives—allows them a place to live in our hearts," writes Ken Gire in *The Reflective Life*. "Without creating spaces of time in our lives, we stunt whatever growth the words were meant to produce."[3]

As someone who works with words, both in speaking and writing, it would be easy for me to fill my life with them. But if those words are going to be authentic, if they are going to live in my heart, I need to give them some space. I need to pause.

"Believers throughout the Bible were used to putting pauses into their lives," Gire continues. "They structured pauses such as set times for daily prayers, strict observances for weekly Sabbaths, and holy days that punctuated the year, such as Passover and Yom Kippur. This habit of structuring pauses made it easier for them to take spontaneous pauses during the day, which is so essential for living a reflective life."[4]

I want to live a reflective life, a simple life, one where God is as close as the air I breathe. I also want to grow stronger in my faith and in my effectiveness. I'm learning that I can do both.

Most of the spiritual practices Jesus modeled for us—solitude, prayer, loving other people—require us to pause. Those moments of rest don't just make life deeper and more reflective. They make us stronger. If you have ever lifted weights, you know that in order to gain muscle strength, you have to rest between sets. As blood pumps through the resting muscle, it is fed and ultimately strengthened.

One reason for pausing is to reflect on what's going on, to do a little self-examination. Self-examination, asking questions about how we are doing spiritually, about what "false self" might drive us to be so hurried, is a spiritual practice that Grace says must be the starting point for slowing down, simplifying, or making any other changes in our lives.

Self-examination is really God-examination. It's asking the question, "What is the truth about me?" and sitting still long enough to listen to God's answer. We discover the joy of being yoked to Jesus when we simply engage in practices like prayer, solitude, listening, loving—things he would do if he were here in our place. Which practices do we need to engage in? If we begin with self-examination, we'll become aware of where we need to grow. If we talk too much, for example, we might need a discipline of silence.

As Grace practiced self-examination, it led her to make pausing a regular practice. Those pauses might be short, like taking the time to say, "I am not in a hurry"; or they might be a bit longer, like an afternoon of solitude. As we do these simple things, as we practice our faith and live as

Jesus would, we meet the Lord, and he tells us, very gently, the truth about ourselves.

Breathing Exercise

Think of something you do several times each day; maybe it's changing diapers or doing dishes. Maybe it's nursing or feeding a baby or throwing a load of laundry into the machine.

Decide that each time you do a repetitive task, you will pause, you will stop, you will breathe—for a full minute, either right before or right after you do it. For example, if you have children in diapers, each time you change a diaper, stop and pause. (If it is a stinky diaper, save the deep breathing until after the baby is changed!) As you clean up your baby, think of how Jesus has taken away the stain of your sin, has cleaned you up. After you've changed your baby, hold him and just breathe for a minute. Don't do anything but pause. Don't hurry on to whatever is next in your day. Stay in this moment, asking God to meet you in it, if only for a brief time. If your kids are older, pause when you help them get dressed, serve them a meal, or whatever. Use this moment to look your children in the eyes and tell them that you love them.

Taking My Own Advice

As I worked on this book, I found myself in conversations with people about the pace of their lives. They would often end up defensive, and I wasn't sure why. But when I stopped to think about it, I noticed something rather ugly in myself.

I was growing a bit smug about the fact that my kids are not overly busy, that I have kept their lives and schedules at a sane pace. I was proud of how they had time to draw, play with Legos, read, or just daydream. My kids were not in too many extracurricular activities. They had time to nurture their creativity. That's good. But while they were nurturing their imaginations, I was beginning to nurture a bit of an attitude, and it wasn't pretty.

My attitude (okay, my snobbiness) didn't endear me to the people I was talking to, especially those who had their kids in four sports. I realized I would need to change my approach if I was going to learn anything about why they chose to live this way. My quiet superiority was creating a barrier.

My pride, however subtle (or not that subtle), also blinded me to another rather ironic problem: although I had set firm limits on my children's schedules, my own commitments were a bit crazy. I was scattered. I was teaching a class at church with a team of three other women, so we had to meet regularly to plan our classes and of course be there every week to teach or to help out. I was involved with teaching at and planning our annual women's retreat at church. I was in a spiritual-formation small group that met every two weeks, and Scot and I were also in a couples' study group. I was speaking outside my church twice a month and always had a major writing project that I was working on. I was serving on the PTA at school and was pretty involved there. I was coaching my daughter's soccer team. I was also playing tennis on a team, which meant I was spending several mornings a week either practicing or playing matches. And then there were those limited things my kids were involved in: I had to spend time driving them to those activities.

My own self-examination brought me to a hard truth: I was scattered, busy, and ever-so-slightly overcommitted. When you become aware of hypocrisy in your own heart, there is a sort of sadness that comes, and also fear: *What if I am found out? What if people realize that the woman writing the book on slowing down is actually too busy?*

I tried to justify myself by saying, "I'm not as bad as I used to be." That was true. And I'm certainly not as busy as a lot of other people. This was also true. But I still have a long way to go. The idea for this book has been growing in my heart for a few years, and I had been slowing down little by little for a long time. But I have to keep slowing down. I have to keep on ruthlessly eliminating hurry, because every day I face pressures to speed up again.

God's been taking me on a long journey, and gradually my pace has been slowing. But my journey isn't over. Just when I thought I had learned enough to write a book on simplicity, my life somehow slipped into a higher gear. It wasn't anything huge, just small things: My husband and I took on a home-renovation project. His business hit the busy season, meaning more of the kid and home responsibilities fell to me. I took on a few extra speaking engagements, some of which required more travel than usual. I had a book to write. I desperately did not want to find myself hurrying to write a book on slowing down. Yet hurry crept in, and to eliminate it, I'd have to ask for help.

In John 15, Jesus said: "I am the true vine and my Father is the gardener. He cuts off every branch in me that bears no fruit, while every branch that does bear fruit he trims clean so that it will be even more fruitful. You are already clean because of the word I have spoken to you. Remain in me, and I will remain in you. No branch can bear fruit by itself; it must remain in the vine. Neither can you bear fruit unless you remain in me. . . . If you obey my commands, you will remain in my love. . . . My command is this: Love each other as I have loved you" (vv. 1–4, 10, 12).

Branches that bear no fruit—did I have any of those in my life? Did you know that if you don't prune a grapevine and just let it sprout all kinds of branches, it won't produce nearly as many grapes as it would if you prune it down to just two branches?

I didn't get this busy overnight; it took awhile. But now I was deeply aware that it was time to allow God to do some gentle pruning.

Breathing Exercise

Reflect on the verses from John 15. Are there branches in your life that don't bear any fruit and don't have potential to do so? Where is God wanting to prune your commitments, your busyness? How does he want you to change your priorities? Change your thinking? Breathe deeply and invite him to make you aware of his presence. Focus solely on the present moment. What do you need to do to remain in God's love at this moment?

Letting God Prune

I had said yes to so many commitments for several reasons: I enjoyed what I was doing and loved the relationships connected with each activity; I got something out of it; I felt success; I felt other people's approval.

But keeping other people happy and working to earn their approval pulled me away from focusing on God and from obeying him.

I knew I had to let God prune away some things that were keeping me from focusing on him. I knew, however, I couldn't just go and quit everything. I had to ask for divine guidance as I tried to settle down. A friend of mine, when I showed her the list of things I was doing, laughed gently but then with great compassion and insight said she thought I suffered from "focus creep." I didn't focus on one thing; my interest and attention crept all over the place. I needed a loving Father's pruning to make my life more fruitful and to get rid of focus creep.

God was gentle, but he did prune. I laid it out for him in my journal; I wrote down everything that I outlined for you a few paragraphs ago, about how scattered my life was. For several months, God had been talking to me about having more time for writing and saying no to other things. I realized I was doing good things, but too many of them, and as a result, they were squeezing out the best things: time with God and time to write.

I agreed I wanted to write. I knew I wasn't giving enough of my time to what God has called me to do. Once I opened myself up to the idea of pruning, some obligations fell away naturally, like coaching soccer (my daughter got better at soccer than me). The difficult discipline lay in not replacing that commitment with another "off-task" obligation. This process took months. I didn't try to hurry my slowing down.

Still, some branches were removed less easily than others. For example, being in several small groups was probably not the best use of my time and energy. I knew I should drop one, but I was afraid. And I wasn't sure how best to be involved with my kids' school. I told God I would need his help in pruning. He obliged. Here's what I wrote after a day he was particularly productive in that task:

> As I sat with my small group this morning, a group of people who have loved and encouraged me for the past six years, I had this picture in my mind of a large pair of pruning shears zeroing in on what was once an important branch of my life and cutting it. As we processed the fact that the group is ending, I saw the shears coming closer. When I

finally admitted out loud that, like others in the group, I think I need to move on and focus on other areas of ministry—especially writing—I felt the pruning shears close around this branch and snip it. The image of the pruned branch falling slowly to earth played like a background tape in my mind.

We prayed at the end of the meeting, then all sat there in a sort of stunned silence. We'd been through so much in six years, and suddenly, the group was a severed stick on the ground of our lives, pruned for our growth, we were sure. Yet, there was a wound, a loss. Jesus's words came to mind: so that it will be even more fruitful. Okay. How is that possible? How can you know you need to let God prune something, yet feel so sad even as you allow it?

Later today, in another conversation, I came to a clear, though surprising, conclusion: next year, I need to take a break from serving on the board of the PTA at my kids' school. Being involved in our public school has been very fruitful. It's solidified relationships with a wide variety of my neighbors and friends, allowed me to keep tabs on what's going on at school, and it's just been fun. It's even opened doors for spiritual conversations with a wide variety of people. It's given me a context and a place to love others, even if I disagreed with them. But it's also been wearying, and frankly, I haven't done a very good job this year of serving the school through my involvement. It's also pulled me away from the work that God has called me to, of writing and teaching. As a result, both my PTA volunteer work and my writing have suffered. As I have tried to open space for God, to listen and to abide, the writing is the clearest calling. Writing is one of the ways I can love people. I tell them what has helped me see God better, and hopefully, as a result, I can provide that same type of vision for others.

Christ's word: love. That is what makes us clean. Listening to his voice of love is what enables us to let go of things that distract us from our true calling.

Breathing Exercise

What keeps you from focusing on Christ? What keeps you from being fully present in each moment of your life? Do you think God might want to prune those things from your life? How do you feel about letting go of those distractions?

10

focused

How can I breathe freely?

In the affluent suburb where Anne and her husband live, overachieving is normal. To keep up, most people are in a hurry. Parents seem to be continually hurrying their kids. "The moms around me are caught up in this culture of going fast," Anne observes. "Their schedules are fast; the kids have to go fast in sports, being on the right team or whatever. They go fast academically. Most of my son's classmates are in summer school, taking things like French, Spanish, or math, to get ready for second grade. That works for them, but it doesn't work for me."

Anne and Jim have three children, ages two, six, and eight. After a lot of prayer and discussion, they decided to go against the grain and not sign up their first grader for the local baseball league, despite the fact that most of the boys in his class were signing up.

"It was practice, plus two games a week," Anne says. "And the games were either from 6:00 to 8:00 p.m. or 8:00 to 10:00 p.m. For first graders! During the school year! I asked the moms if that was hard on the kids and they said, 'Oh, yes, they're a mess at school the next day if they have their game in that 8:00 to 10:00 p.m. slot.'"

Anne wanted her child to have fun and be able to do things with his friends. She and Jim talked about the baseball team and prayed about it. When they talked to other parents, they tried to understand why this was important to them, despite the fact that it kept their children out late on school nights.

"People told me, 'If you don't sign your son up now, he won't get in when he's older.' They operate out of this fear that their child will not fit in, that he'll somehow fall behind," Anne said. "Well, if that's important to them, that's fine. But we don't want to operate out of fear, and we don't want to be out at dinnertime three nights a week. So we decided not to do baseball. All the other moms think I'm nuts."

There is great freedom in saying no, but that doesn't make it easy. But Anne's not just saying no to be negative. She's doing it so she is able to say yes to God.

I've known Anne for years. She's never been one to be pulled along by the culture or peer pressure. She is deliberate about setting some good boundaries. For example, if you call her house, she rarely answers the phone. The answering machine is always on because she screens her calls. Also, she does not have email, so she doesn't have to spend time checking email, answering email, deleting unwanted email. If I really want to email her something, I can email it to her husband at work, but I've found it's easier to call (and leave a message!) or just snail mail it.

These small things are Anne's way of being deliberate, setting boundaries, and making her life a little saner. But she found the culture around her was beginning to make her speed up.

"I felt like I was always in a hurry. I had a healthy craving to go slow," Anne says. "The culture around me goes fast; my husband's job goes fast. In my parenting, I was noticing things I didn't like. I was starting to focus on things like keeping the house clean rather than just hanging out with my kids. Life felt sort of stressful. I wanted a better marriage and better parenting. Jim and I had a good marriage, but I felt like life was getting hurried and it could be stronger."

Anne fought to keep her life sane, but it wasn't easy. She admits she likes being in charge and keeping things in order. Sometimes that causes her to hurry. When he was young, her eldest child developed a bit of a stutter. She fretted over it; then finally it occurred to her to ask him what he thought was going on.

"Mommy, you go so fast," her son replied. "You only give me a little time to answer and I can't get the words out fast enough."

That moment with her son, Anne says, was God's way of telling her, "You have to change."

Despite the push of her peers, God has given Anne some strong directions on slowing and simplifying her life. Certainly, that conversation with her eldest was one example. Another message came with the birth of her third baby.

John was a beautiful baby, but as he grew that first year, Anne could tell something was off. His development didn't match the milestones in *What to Expect the First Year*. At nine months old, he couldn't crawl, sit up, or stand. After numerous tests and doctor visits, he was diagnosed with "low tone," which means his muscles did not develop the way they should. His muscle tone was simply a lot lower than other children his age.

Little John began a rigorous course of physical therapy, which required Anne or Jim to work with him every day to develop the "memory" in his muscles. They'd sit him up, for example, and when he started to fall, he didn't know how to catch himself. The reflex that most children quickly develop just wasn't there. So they'd catch him and move his muscles for him, to teach the muscles how to move to achieve balance. The time Anne had to spend caring for him, working with him, taking him to the doctor, in addition to caring for her other two children, forced her to slow down.

"We knew having another baby would throw us into chaos. But we also knew it would make us depend on God," Anne said. "I really think God gave this condition to John for me. I already wanted to slow down. In John, God gave me an excuse. I needed it. But I didn't know how."

Anne asked God to show her what her next step ought to be. She sensed that intentional simplicity might be a lighter burden than hurry. "One night I was in the tub, just relaxing, and God gave me a plan for slowing down, a way to feed that healthy craving," Anne said.

The four things that came to her mind were:

1. Go slow.
2. Live simply.
3. Live in the present.
4. Live in reality.

God brought these four simple rules to her mind, and she has spent the last couple of years trying to learn what it means to live them out.

"I want a good family," Anne says. "I want a level of parenting that's better than the status quo. It's not popular to go slow, but I want to enjoy my children. For the last couple of years, I've been going at a slower pace, keeping these four things in mind."

Anne says she has to keep reminding herself that these directives are not about living a perfect life but about keeping focused on Jesus.

"Jesus is my model in all of these steps," she says. "He did all four things. He went slow, lived simply, lived in the moment, and was never in denial. So when other people think I'm crazy for living the way I do, I just look at Jesus. The most powerful person in my life is Jesus. He can help me walk each of these roads."

Four Steps to Freedom

God has always called his people to be a light in the darkness. In our hurried-up, stressed-out world, here is what an extremely bright light looks like: a slow pace, a simple life, being present, being real.

Anne's first rule of life, "Go slow," is countercultural, especially in the town where she lives. "I ask people, why are you rushing? Why are you putting your two-year-old in ballet class? I mean, I really want to know. But they don't know. They just say, 'Well, everyone is in ballet, so my kid should be too.' They don't think about it. I think it's because if you go slow, you have to feel stuff. I think people go fast to avoid feeling their emotions, dealing with their junk."

Anne has spent some time going slow and noticed that it did give her more time to think about her life, her emotions. Like many who have chosen to travel in the slow lane of life, she's found some of those emotions were painful, and it was helpful to process those feelings with a counselor.

Not an easy task, but one that has ultimately brought great freedom and joy. Anne has found that she's grown more by going slow, and she's become more mindful about her life and what she wants. She no longer does things just because everyone else is doing them.

Hurry is a great way to avoid whatever issues you wrestle with. But wouldn't it be great if you could be healthy, if you could really love God without your fear and anxiety and issues getting in the way? Anne is moving toward that kind of health (she'd be the first to tell you that you never really *arrive*) by going slower.

Anne's second practice was to determine what steps she needed to take to "live simply." What does that mean? It looks different in each life. I can't spell it out for you. You have to listen to God yourself. That may seem like a bummer. But actually it's also the bonus. You *get to* listen to God. If I gave you three easy steps, you would miss out on experiencing God's guidance for yourself, and that is something you don't want to miss. You've had a glimpse into the lives of the women on these pages. As you read this book, where did you say, *I want that*? Sometimes God speaks to us through that type of longing. If God doesn't talk to you in the bathtub, don't worry. Maybe he's speaking to you through the stories in this book, and your next step might be to choose just one thing that one person in this book has done and see how it fits into your life. That could be the start of your Sabbath Simplicity journey.

"We live in a culture that is very materialistic," Anne notes. "I see some of these women around me, at my son's school. Their husbands are workaholics, they have nice homes and everything money can buy, but they are lonely. They buy their kids whatever they ask for. But they don't really think about how a choice like that will form their child's character.

"I intentionally parent with Jim. We go out on date nights; we talk about parenting, about where the kids are involved, what they need from us as parents, where we need to let them try things on their own, where they need our help."

Simple living for Anne and her children means not too many summer activities, although she let her eight-year-old enroll in a park district football camp. "He was so excited about it," she says. "Right now I'm trying to notice—what is his passion, what does he really like? I'm trying to listen and go with that."

The other day, she took her kids to the candy store, where they each were able to select a treat. This was an entire afternoon's outing, and the kids were excited because it was not a regular trip for them. Rather than swim team or swim lessons, she takes them to the community pool and plays in the water with them. She intentionally tries to keep the summer calm and slow.

Simplicity also means not overspending, especially spending to keep up with the other kids in the neighborhood or at school. It means home birthday parties rather than expensive parties at migraine-producing places like amusement parks or game arcade/pizza places. Anne said her son told her that all the kids in his class were talking about his birthday party. Worried, she asked what they had said about having cake and presents and Pin the Tail on the Donkey at home, having just a few friends instead of thirty kids at the party. "They said mine was the best party!" her son proclaimed.

Living simply also means, for Anne, not scheduling every minute of her children's day, allowing them to build their imagination. In order for that to happen, she has to let them figure out what to do. That can be hard when the kids complain that they are bored. But she's found that if she simply and gently refuses to entertain them or solve their boredom problem, they will launch into some imaginative game. Because many parents don't want to endure the few moments of whining, they miss the payoff. "It's so fun to see the kids playing together and building their creativity," she says.

I've found this to be true with my own kids. When they say, "I'm bored," I simply look at them sympathetically and say, "Well, you have a problem, don't you? I think you can solve your problem if you try." And usually they do.

Since Anne's children have plenty of time to practice getting along, they have learned how to do it. The learning process is often more difficult for the parents than for the children. We want to step in and solve their problems, make them happy, whatever. We do them a great disservice by interfering in this way, I think. Learning from their mistakes, learning how to get along without a parent refereeing every minute, develops invaluable life skills in children.

Going slow and living simply also means family meals, where Anne and Jim teach their kids about love and respect, about how to carry on a conversation. They teach by practicing it at the dinner table.

"When our kids are grown, why would they want to come back for family dinners on holidays if they don't have the memory of regular family meals during their childhood?" Anne asks.

Anne's third credo, "Live in the present," builds on the first two. "If you're not slow and simple, you can't live in the moment," Anne notes. "And if you want to enjoy a person, you have to be present with them, be in the moment."

Her husband does strategic planning in his job, and one time he asked her, "Why did we have kids?" He wasn't frustrated with them or regretting their decision to raise a family. He was thinking strategically. His answer to his own question: "To enjoy them." Going slowly, living simply, and living in the present allows them to do just that, to enjoy their children before their childhood rushes by in a flurry of activity and busyness. To do that, the couple needs to be in the present.

Anne says living in the present is hard because we're so often wanting to achieve and figure things out. That kind of thinking puts us in the future rather than the moment. To live in the present, we have to let go of trying to control things a bit. We have to give more energy to paying attention than we do to trying to control. For most of us, including Anne, that's hard.

Her final goal is to "live in reality, not in denial." For Anne, this meant "coming out of denial about my emotional junk. I want to work through it so I don't harm my kids and so my marriage is a good one."

Anne realized that unless she faced up to her own shortcomings, she would create stress in her home. She spent time with a counselor taking a realistic look at how she grew up and how her personality has developed. She faced the truth about her strengths and also her woundedness.

Living in reality meant she needed to ponder how she was raised, how she wants to emulate some of the things her parents did and change the things she wishes had been different. She spent time grieving things that she regrets, things she never had but wished she did. She worked at being honest and real, not pretending that she had it all together when she didn't. She sees that as a process that continues throughout life.

"I'm working toward what God made me to be," she says. "I realize I can be kind of controlling. I'm trying to back off, but that's hard."

Anne found a Bible verse for each of her four areas and wrote them down to remind her to keep her focus on God and his direction. She has found that while she is not much of a journal keeper, just writing down verses that resonate with her has created a record of God's work in her life. "I copy down verses that mean a lot to me, and then I'll go back sometimes and read them, reflect on them. It doesn't feel overwhelming that way, and it connects my experiences with God's Word."

She and her husband have also started being intentional about resting on Sundays. "We go to church; we come home. We don't have soccer, so we can just hang with the kids. We've just decided we're not going there, because we think this is a saner way to live." In other words, they've said no to soccer in order to say yes to sanity. Sounds like a good trade-off. But the choices of yes and no are not arbitrary. She and her husband are trying to listen to God, to find the freedom that comes in that.

"Jesus is the focus," she says. "I don't know how I could do it without him. God gave me this outline, but it would all be unattainable without him in my life."

Breathing Exercise

Take a few minutes to breathe deeply and slowly. How do you respond to Anne's story? Do you live in a "culture of going fast" as Anne says she does? How do you respond to that culture? Which of the four rules that Anne lives by do you most deeply desire to incorporate into your own life? What small step could you take toward that desire?

Directed by the Lord

As you can see, Anne used her own unique style to incorporate practices such as meditating on Scripture, journaling, prayer, self-examination, and Sabbath-keeping into her life. That's helped her keep her focus on God and live into the directions God had given her.

Another important discipline that we sometimes don't label as "spiritual" but has everything to do with our spiritual growth is simply "saying yes and saying no." Anne and her husband are being intentional about seeking God's direction, not just about big "spiritual" issues but small daily decisions as well. God wants to be involved in all of our decisions. As the psalmist says, "The steps of the godly are directed by the LORD. He delights in every detail of their lives" (Ps. 37:23 NLT).

Do you believe that God delights in the details of your life? Are you willing to carefully consider what to say yes and no to and let the Lord direct you in that? Do you believe doing that will bring you freedom?

We often think of spiritual disciplines as being things like solitude, prayer, study, and meditation. And indeed, these are disciplines that can help us grow closer to God, as we see from Anne. Yet they might not. If we pile hours of prayer and Bible study onto a life that is already too busy, these disciplines will not help us at all. Intimacy with God can't be created in a hurry.

Do you believe this? Or do you think that you'll have more time for God if you simply do everything else a little faster?

If that's how you do your life, I have a Dr. Phil–type question for you: How's that working for you? Do you experience deep inner peace and an intimate connection with God? Does hurrying the other parts of your life really free up more time for God? How's the quality of that time? Does that feel like an easy yoke, a light burden?

M. Shawn Copeland, associate professor of theology at Marquette University, writes: "If we are to grow in faithful living, we need to renounce the things that choke off the fullness of life that God intended for us, and we must follow through on our commitments to pray, to be conscientious, and to be in mutually supportive relations with other faithful persons. These acts take self-discipline. We must learn the practice of saying no to that which crowds God out and yes to a way of life that makes space for God."[1]

If we slow down enough to listen to God's direction and pray for his help in deciding what to say no to, we can strengthen our spiritual lives in two ways: first, we grow in deeper connection with him by simply listening and obeying; and second, we will hopefully say no to things that pull us away from him.

Copeland continues: "Do I understand that each choice I make influences the choices I can make in the future? Do I understand that in saying yes to every invitation or opportunity, every task or assignment, I limit the possibilities for my growth in other areas?"[2]

Sometimes, I have to say no to my friends, my spouse, even my kids, in order to say yes to God. To grow closer to him, I need times of quiet, reflection, rest. I need Sabbath Simplicity.

As I speak to parents about the pace of their lives, a recurring theme emerges. People who feel as if their lives are moving too fast but aren't sure why have this in common: they rarely say no.

But when we always say yes to demands of others, we are automatically saying no to something. Maybe to God, maybe to our kids. If I say yes, for example, to attend a meeting at school or church, I am saying, "No, I can't be with my family that evening. Someone other than me will have to take care of things at home at that time."

Sometimes that is fine. But be aware that every yes (and every no) has a price, a trade-off.

Breathing Exercise

Are you living a way of life that makes space for God? Or have you said yes to too many things? What consequences might that have? What are some things that "choke off the fullness of life that God intended" for you? What kind of life do you think he intends for you to have? What would you have to do differently to "say no to that which crowds God out"?

Saying No to Overscheduling

If your children are very small, you may not be tempted to involve them in a lot of activities. Trust me, the day is coming. It's good to set some boundaries ahead of time, because if you don't choose Jesus's yoke, you will (perhaps unintentionally) pick up the yoke of the world, the one that says, "You have to do this or you'll fall behind. You have to go here or you won't be well-liked or accepted." You'll find yourself trapped in a yoke of hurry.

Hurry keeps us from paying attention to where Christ is leading us. The reverse is also true: paying attention to him keeps us from hurrying. But it's hard to pay attention when so many voices call out to us in seemingly innocuous ways: do this, try this, buy this, have this, sign up for this. The life Jesus calls us to is one where we don't find our self-worth in activity but rather in connection with him.

Dorothy Bass writes, "Gaining time for attention to God and to my family means figuring out where to say no on a daily basis."[3]

That gets harder as your kids get older, especially in our culture that values competition and achievement. But thinking and deciding what you want your schedule and pace to look like before the opportunities come up will often make the choices easier.

When a child is already involved in several extracurricular activities and asks her parent if she can sign up for another, it is often appropriate for the parent to say no. Not because that particular activity is bad but because too many activities can crowd God out.

"She says she can handle it," one mom told me as she signed her child up for yet another sport. The question is not whether a child—who does not have her driver's license and does not wash her own uniforms or cook her own meals—can "handle it." The question you need to ask is whether you as a parent can handle it and whether you as a family can handle it. And you need to ask the child that as well. Good parenting involves asking your child to grapple with questions such as, "What will adding one more sport to my schedule do to my mom? What will it do to our family? Will we have dinner together more often as a family, or less often, as a result of my choice?"

What character trait do these questions teach a child? Unselfishness. This would seem to be a far more valuable lesson for your child than learning lacrosse at age six!

If we fail to ask these questions, we deny our children the opportunity to "put away childish things," such as self-centeredness. In his book *The Purpose-Driven Life*, Rick Warren tells his readers that if they want a life with purpose and meaning, they must first accept this foundational truth: "It's not about you."

For many people, this is a brand-new concept. Do your children know that it's not about them? I remember once getting frustrated with my daughter when she was two. "You are not the center of the universe," I told her as she raged. "Yes, I am!" she replied quickly. This is very normal for a two-year-old. Good parents keep repeating the "You are not the center of the universe" mantra until it sticks. If you never set limits or say no, you are, in effect, telling your child he is the center of the universe.

Do your kids know how to make decisions based on the fact that they are part of a family, a community, a world? And that their decisions have an impact on that world? They might be able to "handle" a busy schedule, but how does that impact the younger sibling who has to spend most evenings in his car seat, eating McDonald's french fries as he rides along in the car pool? How does it impact the soul of their mother, who fears that her rear end will meld with the driver's seat of the minivan if she spends one more hour driving her children around in it?

Many parents are afraid that saying no will somehow damage their children or cause resentment. Never saying no will cause far more damage, not just to your children, but also to the people who have to live with them down the road. Fast-forward in your mind: *What kind of person will my child become?*

Do you want your daughter to marry a man who has never learned about limits? Will he be faithful to the loving limits of marriage? Do you want your son to marry a girl who has never learned limits? Will she be able to stay within the limits of their budget when she visits the mall?

Do you want your son to grow up not knowing how to say no, so that when he goes to work for a man who continually piles work on him, he doesn't know how to say, "Enough"? If your child grows up to be that boss, and you've never set limits, how will he know how to say no? If you've always asked, "How high, sweetie?" when he says, "Jump," what kind of boss do you think he will be?

A child without limits at home often has trouble dealing with the limits imposed by school or workplace. Wouldn't we want to prepare our children for success not by providing them with endless "opportunities" but rather with loving limits that take the well-being of others into consideration?

I'm not saying you shouldn't tell your child he's wonderful and that you love him. Don't limit your love. Just don't confuse giving a child everything he thinks he wants with love.

Our society values individuality and personal fulfillment over the good of the group and, consequentially, confuses needs and wants.

If Johnny wants to play four sports, does that mean he should? I want things too, but that doesn't mean I should have them. For example, I want a live-in maid and nanny. I could have them, but at what price? The cost—in terms of dollars and in terms of opportunities to build my character by hard work and hands-on parenting—is one I choose not to pay. I have a choice. And you do too. You may say, "A maid is not even a choice for me." Yes, it is. You could choose to hire a housekeeper instead of buying groceries or paying the rent. Obviously, that would be a foolish choice. But so often we indulge the wants of our children and don't even look at the price tag. It's higher than you think.

Where do the "shoulds" like that come from? Sometimes they come from our friends, family, spouse. Your husband may think music is important, or sports. Maybe you have signed up your child for tutoring or academic enrichment courses because you desire him to be a high achiever. Why do you need that? Maybe you have preconceived notions of what kids should do. Maybe you want your kids to achieve things you didn't. Or maybe things you did achieve. You want them to be a little you. But often they are not.

My husband, pre-kids, wanted to have a son. "Why is that important?" I asked, my feminist hackles rising. "So I can have someone to do sports with," he replied. He grew up loving sports, spending most of his time playing basketball and tennis. "Can't you do sports with a daughter?" I asked. "Well . . ." he said, trying to imagine it.

God definitely has a sense of humor. Our son has gamely tried a variety of sports. The one he likes best is golf. But he is much more interested in artistic and intellectual pursuits than in athletic ones. At this stage in his development, that's where his strengths lie. That may change as he grows older, but for now, that's where he's at.

Our daughter, on the other hand, loves sports. She is eager to talk about the World Series or the Super Bowl or other sporting events, loves playing soccer, won't wear dresses, watches football games with her daddy and discusses them with the boys at the bus stop the next morning. Her current "When I grow up" aspiration is to be a sports announcer on television. If anyone is "doing sports" with Scot, it's Melanie.

The Bible tells us, "Train up a child in the way he should go." It does not say, "in the way you think he ought to go" or "the way so you can live out your unfulfilled dreams." A closer translation of this text might render it, "Raise a child according to his or her particular bent." Children are like vines; we need to prune and direct them, but ultimately, we need to pay attention to how God created them and lovingly direct their growth according to the gifts and abilities God has placed within them.

Moms at Play

So, how did God create *you*? Are you growing according to the gifts and abilities God has placed within you?

Living in Sabbath Simplicity requires paying attention to how God created us—our gifts, our strengths, our personalities. When God made you, he didn't look at you, sigh, and say, "Oh, well." He said, "YES! That's exactly what I meant to do." What are you doing to develop the gifts and abilities he's given you?

As parents, we can often become consumed with doing things for our kids, with our kids, because of our kids.

I have found, though, that I am a better mom if I do some things for me, without the kids. I need opportunities to play. For me, that means athletic activity. It could be an aerobics class or going jogging, but I find that athletic competition suits my personality and strengths.

Why? One, it's good exercise and strong motivation. I'm much more motivated if I am exercising for a purpose other than fitting into my jeans. If my workouts lead to a situation where I can compete and actually win, that's much more interesting than simply being able to master a new step in a Jazzercise class.

Two, I often find that because I have a bit of a competitive nature, I tend to get a little overenthused when I'm watching my kids play sports. I try to achieve through them, which doesn't work and stresses all of us out considerably. If I have an outlet for my competitive energy, I'm less likely to get so hyper on the sidelines.

One year, I signed up for an indoor soccer league for adults. This gave new meaning to the term "soccer moms." We were moms playing soccer, a bunch of thirtysomething former athletes, sweating and gasping, realizing that actually running around and kicking a ball is definitely harder than it looks when you are sitting in your captain's chair on the sidelines, sipping a diet Coke and yelling at your first grader.

If you find yourself yelling at your kids too much at sporting events, sign up for even one session of soccer or some other league sport. It will give you a good workout and raise your empathy level a few notches. Scot and the kids came to a couple of my games. Melanie asked tentatively, "Can I yell at you?" I knew this had been an issue between us: I had been doing more than my share of yelling on the sidelines at *her* soccer games, so I agreed. She found great delight in yelling from the sidelines, "Go to that ball, Mommy! Get going! Kick it!"

While it wasn't easy, playing soccer was fun. It was good for my body and my mind; it gave me something to think about besides my kids and their world.

Eventually, I turned to tennis, which is my current sport (I'm getting older, okay?). I'm on a team that practices a few times a week while the kids are at school. It's given me some new friends and a new confidence (it's not as physically demanding as soccer).

If your kid is in three activities and you are in zero, that's not unselfish of you. It's unbalanced. If you don't like sports, take a class in something you're interested in—maybe scrapbooking or sewing or photography. Take piano lessons. Join a book club or a Bible study. Read a book for fun. You should have a chance to do something fun, a chance to play, without your kids. I'm not saying you should do all these things, or you'll be back to being hurried. But be sure your schedule includes some playtime for you—even if that means just going to the public library alone for an hour and getting lost in a good novel.

If your kids are small, you may have to get a sitter or leave them with your husband for an hour or two. This is not just okay, this is necessary. Living in Sabbath Simplicity means you make time for you.

Breathing Exercise

Sit quietly and take a few slow breaths. What kinds of things do you do to play without your kids? If you don't have any interests outside of the kids, spend some time thinking about why that is. If you find yourself resisting this idea, sit with that resistance for a while. Where does it come from? What are you afraid of?

Make a list of activities, sports, or classes you might be interested in if you had the time. Brainstorm ideas. Don't edit yourself; just write whatever comes to mind. Now look at your list. Which one will you give yourself permission to explore further? What could you do to make the time for yourself?

The Family That Plays Together . . .

Our culture tends to put parents on the sidelines and kids on the field. But it doesn't have to be that way. Physical activities (from taking a walk to downhill skiing) can be a great way for a family to spend time together.

Take your children on a bike ride or a walk through your neighborhood. Play catch in the yard with them. Take a walk to the park and actually go down the slide with them. Play tag with them.

In winter, the hill next to our kids' elementary school is a favorite sledding spot. My kids love to coast down the hill on their sleds, but they love it even more when I climb on the sled with them.

If you crave structure (or just want some interaction with other people), take a class with your kids. Don't just drop them off somewhere. Sign up for a class or sport lesson (say tennis, golf, photography, whatever) that you can do with your child. If you have a baby, take an exercise class that includes mothers and infants.

One of my favorite memories of my junior high years (and those years have very few good memories for me!) was going horseback riding with my mom. Outside of that realm, we were sometimes close, but sometimes we clashed, as preteen girls and their mothers tend to do. When we drove to the stable and took a riding lesson together, though, we got along really well (I think in part because it was the one place I didn't feel awkward but also because I had time to just hang out with her). We'd ride together, then stop on the way home for ice cream. Our shared interest built a rapport that strengthened our connection with each other.

I know some parents who take Tae Kwon Do with their children, others who simply enjoy camping, biking, or hiking together. Family activities don't have to be expensive or all-consuming.

A life of Sabbath Simplicity is not about withdrawing from people; it is a life lived in the context of community, especially the community of our family. Neither is it a life without any activity; it is an unhurried life engaged in a rhythm of meaningful activity and times of rest. Saying no to hurry allows us to say yes to giving our attention and love to our family and yes to the joy that comes from focusing on what really matters.

Breathing Exercise

Talk to your family and choose a sport or activity that you can all learn and enjoy together. If you are not particularly athletic, try having a family board-game night or try simply walking around the block together. Don't hurry. Notice bugs, leaves, flowers, and the people in your neighborhood. Stop to talk to a neighbor. Take time to notice what it is that your kids notice. The things that are important to them may escape your attention.

afterword

the next step

As I sit down to write this last chapter, I have to ask: so, what have you learned?

To be honest, I'm not asking you, I'm asking me. What have I learned after talking to all these women, hearing their stories, watching how God has worked and led and shaped their lives and souls? Although they have a lot in common, each of these moms is unique. Each one is following God as he leads. None of them is completely "done" with their journey toward simplicity; they are simply taking some steps. Steps unique to them, directed by God. Those steps are not the same for everyone. You won't get far living a Sabbath Simplicity life if you approach it as if it were the latest diet, where just following the rules and recipes will get you the results you want (or at least tell you what choices are acceptable).

The danger in these stories is that you will focus on the differences between your life and the lives of these women. You may feel you could certainly simplify if you didn't have a demanding career, or an unsupportive (or unemployed) spouse, or a child with physical or emotional challenges, or . . . (fill in your blank). Because of your circumstances, you just can't.

While I've told you the stories of real moms in part to show you how they have simplified, you won't be able to precisely duplicate what they have done. That's okay. No matter what the circumstances of your life are, you can think about your next step. That step could be as big as a career change or as small as remembering to take a deep breath before you speak each time you are angry.

Simplicity is not a method. At its heart, simplicity is a relationship with God that is focused on him and is growing, changing, evolving.

Many well-intentioned people asked if I was going to include tips on meal-planning, organization, filing systems, and housecleaning in this book. Sorry. There are many books on systems of all kinds, many helpful tips in magazines and websites and other places. They have their place, but they are the next step after you've dealt with the heart of the issue, which is your heart.

Is your heart divided? You can organize and downscale all you want, but if your heart is not focused on Jesus, you won't live a simple life.

I have a friend who has a painful life. In part, because she wrestles with physical health problems and loneliness, but also because she carries a burden of envy and anger that she does not have a different life. She asks herself, Why don't I have the money some other people have? Why don't I get to have physical health that other people seem to take for granted? Why can't I have the relationships some other people have, or the success or love that other people enjoy?

If you spend a lot of time thinking about what you don't have, especially in regard to material possessions, money is your god—perhaps even more than someone who has great material wealth. If you focus on what you don't have relationally or vocationally, then you can't add on simplicity and hope it will solve your problems.

Such thoughts are a burden that will sink your soul and distract your heart from all that God wants to give you.

As I wrote in part 2, the practice of simplicity has to do with our focus. But the world seems to be increasingly scattered, increasingly distracting. It's hard for me to focus on anything, especially on Jesus; I'm tempted to focus on what I don't have. But when I turn my eyes to Jesus and really focus on him and all he is to me, all the distractions and difficulties of parenting, work, friendships, and marriage fall into place.

Not that all my problems or challenges disappear. They just get put into proper perspective. I see them *through* Jesus, with Jesus. In the context of that relationship, I have a companion to walk beside me, yoked to me, who bears the burdens with me. He is the only one who loves me perfectly. My spouse, my parents, my kids, and my friends love me, but just as I love them—imperfectly. They *can't* love me perfectly. They're human. But Jesus loves me perfectly.

Simplicity puts the focus on that love relationship, and when we make decisions based on that relationship, we might choose the same things many of the women in this book chose. Our motive, however, will be listening to Jesus, not figuring out and copying the methods of others.

When I am looking at Jesus, I can access his wisdom about my life rather than being distracted from him by my life.

Still, combining the practices of slowing and simplicity with parenting in the twenty-first century is a challenge. I would never attempt it without a lot of prayer. And that is another thing I have learned. Prayer is essential to eliminating hurry and simplifying. You may be in a stage of life or of parenting where you think: *Pray? I don't have time to pray.* And you may be right. You may have chosen to live at a pace that doesn't leave room for prayer, especially if you think prayer is sitting and reading a shopping list to God.

I'm not talking about "gimme" prayers or even long-winded confessions or intercessions for others. Rather, I'm talking about prayer that brings us into God's presence and then simply listens for his direction. Prayer that is like breathing in the presence of God.

When I pray this way, God will sometimes direct me to shed things or activities I don't need so I can more easily participate in what God is doing in this world. He will invite me to simplify: to stop looking at other people or things, to throw off that which encumbers, to be able to move freely but in obedience to him. When I am fully focused on Jesus and his amazing love for me, I want to listen to him. I want to please him.

"Prayer is the act by which the people of God become incorporated into the presence and action of God in the world," writes Robert Mulholland. "Prayer becomes a sacrificial offering of ourselves to God, to become agents of God's presence and action in the daily events and situations of our lives. How different this is from the idea of prayer as asking God to change our situation without any involvement on our part!"[1]

When you love your children, when you play with them or discipline them, you can see it as something that crowds out room for prayer. Or you can see that, in the daily tasks of parenting, you are offering yourself sacrificially to God, attempting to "become [an agent] of God's presence and action." That is, you are praying.

Prayer is like breathing. (Sound familiar?!) If you have done the Breathing Exercises, you will have become more comfortable with slowing down and being mindful and present. You'll know that these practices of Sabbath-keeping slowing and simplicity are not add-ons to life; they simply are life. They are the life-giving way of life that Jesus invites us into when he says, "Come to me."

A life of Sabbath Simplicity calls us to be in the moment but also to be intentional about how we live our days. To be focused, yet open. To find a way of life, but freedom within it. It doesn't mean spending several hours a day having a "quiet time." It means cultivating a quiet spirit throughout your day and noticing God all the time, not just in the allotted time slot you've given him in your day timer.

In other words, Sabbath Simplicity is about learning what Eugene Peterson calls "the unforced rhythms of grace." Look at how he translates Jesus's invitation that we've been looking at through this book: "Are you tired? Worn out? Burned out on religion? Come to me. Get away with me and you'll recover your life. I'll show you how to take a real rest. Walk with me and work with me—watch how I do it. Learn the unforced rhythms of grace. I won't lay anything heavy or ill-fitting on you. Keep company with me and you'll learn to live freely and lightly" (Matt. 11:28–30 Message).

Read that again. Doesn't that sound appealing? Sometimes my life, even the stuff I label my "spiritual life," makes me feel tired and burned out. I'm looking for "a real rest." I want to recover my life.

Do you feel free and light? Do you feel like you can dance to unforced rhythms? Or are you rather awkward?

Do you feel weary and burdened? "Burned out on religion" as Peterson translates it? Is the image of God you carry around in your heart one of someone gentle and humble? Or does he seem a taskmaster, or perhaps a heavenly Father with rather high expectations of you?

Jesus is offering us a lifestyle. A way of life: living freely and lightly. Jesus's yoke is not something we have to bear alone. It's the life he's inviting us to share with him, and it's not a burden, it's a way of living that would result in spiritual transformation.

If we want to act as Jesus would, to love others and be present with them in the way he did, to be as unhurried as he was, we need to emulate him. Not just his knowledge, wisdom, teachings. We need to order our lives in much the same way that he did, to engage in the practices he did.

Many of the women whose stories you've read have found the place where they can look at Jesus and see him in the midst of parenting, in the midst of their busy, or not so busy, lives. And that is enough. They are content, not because of their circumstances but because they have chosen contentment regardless of their circumstances.

I have chosen the unforced rhythms of grace that Jesus offers through Sabbath Simplicity. My hope is that you will too.

God is as close as the air you breathe. We can choose to live life gasping and grasping. Or we can breathe deeply . . . and experience his simple, restful presence.

notes

Introduction

1. Thomas R. Kelly, *A Testament of Devotion* (1941; repr. New York: Harper-Collins, 1992), 72.
2. Ibid.

Chapter 1: Hurried and Worried

1. Brent W. Bost, M.D., http://www.hurriedwoman.com.
2. John Ortberg, *The Life You've Always Wanted* (Grand Rapids: Zondervan, 1997), 81–82.
3. Richard A. Swenson, M.D., *Margin: Restoring Emotional, Physical, Financial and Time Reserves to Overloaded Lives* (Colorado Springs: NavPress, 1992), 16.
4. Ibid., 91–92.

Chapter 2: Out of Breath

1. David Elkind, *The Hurried Child: Growing Up Too Fast Too Soon* (Cambridge, MA: Perseus, 2001), 40.
2. Ibid., 34.
3. Ibid., xi.
4. Ibid., 32–33.

Chapter 3: Scattered

1. Verna Noel Jones, "Manage Your Stress," Resources, *Chicago Tribune*, June 27, 2004.

Chapter 4: Simplified

1. Richard Foster, *Freedom of Simplicity* (New York: HarperCollins, 1981), 45.

2. Duane Elgin, *Voluntary Simplicity: Toward a Way of Life That Is Outwardly Simple, Inwardly Rich* (New York: William Morrow, 1993), 25.

3. Ibid., 43.

4. Joe Dominguez and Vicki Robin, *Your Money or Your Life: Transforming Your Relationship with Money and Achieving Financial Independence* (New York: Penguin, 1992), 79.

5. Ibid., 79.

6. Keri Wyatt Kent, *God's Whisper in a Mother's Chaos* (Downers Grove, IL: InterVarsity, 2000), 70.

Chapter 5: Mindful

1. Henry Cloud and John Townsend, *Boundaries with Kids* (Grand Rapids: Zondervan, 1998).

2. Randy Frazee, *Making Room for Life: Trading Chaotic Lifestyles for Connected Relationships* (Grand Rapids: Zondervan, 2003), 77.

3. From an article by Vijai P. Sharma, "Family Meals Strengthen Family Bonds," Mind Publications, 2001. www.mindpub.com.

4. The website www.abcnews.com is just one of many that offers information on family meals. Google "family meals" and you'll find all kinds of very helpful information. Also www.Webmd.com and other health sites often have articles on the topic, which experts continue to realize is related to children's physical and emotional health.

Chapter 6: Humble

1. Wayne Muller, *Sabbath: Restoring the Sacred Rhythm of Rest* (New York: Bantam, 1999), 2.

2. Parker Palmer, *Let Your Life Speak* (San Francisco: Jossey-Bass, 2000), 4.

Chapter 7: Rested

1. Marjorie Thompson, *Soul Feast* (Louisville: Westminster John Knox, 1995), 58.

2. Dorothy Bass, *Receiving the Day* (San Francisco: Jossey-Bass, 2000), 48.

Chapter 8: Sheltered

1. Muller, *Sabbath: Restoring the Sacred Rhythm of Rest*, 8.

2. Ibid., 25-26.

Chapter 9: Slow

1. Richard Carlson and Joseph Bailey, *Slowing Down to the Speed of Life* (San Francisco: HarperSanFrancisco, 1997), xxii.
2. Ibid., 68.
3. Ken Gire, *The Reflective Life* (Colorado Springs: Chariot Victor, 1998), 43.
4. Ibid.

Chapter 10: Focused

1. M. Shawn Copeland, *Practicing Our Faith*, ed. Dorothy Bass (San Francisco: Jossey-Bass, 1997), 60.
2. Ibid., 70.
3. Bass, *Receiving the Day*, 39.

Afterword

1. Robert Mulholland Jr., *Invitation to a Journey: A Road Map for Spiritual Formation* (Downers Grove, IL: InterVarsity, 1993), 108.

the MOPS story

You take care of your children, Mom. Who takes care of you? MOPS International (Mothers of Preschoolers) provides mothers of preschoolers with the nurture and resources they need to be the best moms they can be.

MOPS is dedicated to the message that "mothering matters" and that moms of young children need encouragement during these critical and formative years. Groups meet in more than 3,200 churches and Christian ministries throughout the United States and in 30 other countries. Each MOPS program helps mothers find friendship and acceptance, provides opportunities for women to develop and practice leadership skills in the group, and promotes spiritual growth. MOPS groups are chartered ministries of local churches and meet at a variety of times and locations: daytime, evenings, and on weekends; in churches, homes, and workplaces.

The MOPPETS program offers a loving learning experience for children while their moms attend MOPS. Other MOPS resources include *MOMSense* magazine and radio, the MOPS International website, and books and resources available through the MOPShop.

With 14.3 million mothers of preschoolers in the United States alone, many moms can't attend a local MOPS group. These moms still need the support that MOPS International can offer. For a small registration fee, any mother of preschoolers can join the MOPS♥to♥Mom Connection and receive *MOMSense* magazine six times a year, a weekly Mom-E-mail message of encouragement, and other valuable benefits.

Find out how MOPS International can help you become part of the MOPS♥to♥Mom Connection and/or join or start a MOPS group. Visit our website at www.mops.org. Phone us at 303-733-5353. Or email Info@mops.org. To learn how to start a MOPS group, call 1-888-910-MOPS.

Keri Wyatt Kent is the author of *God's Whisper in a Mother's Chaos* and *The Garden of the Soul*. She writes and speaks often on spiritual formation and growth. She lives with her husband and two children in Hoffman Estates, Illinois. More information about her ministry is available on www.keriwyattkent.com.